THE LEGACIES OF
JULIUS NYERERE

THE LEGACIES OF
JULIUS NYERERE
INFLUENCES ON DEVELOPMENT
DISCOURSE AND PRACTICE IN AFRICA

EDITED by
David McDonald
and
Eunice Njeri Sahle

Africa World Press, Inc.

P.O. Box 1892
Trenton, NJ 08607

P.O. Box 48
Asmara, ERITREA

Africa World Press, Inc.

P.O. Box 1892
Trenton, NJ 08607

P.O. Box 48
Asmara, ERITREA

Copyright © 2002 David A. McDonald and Eunice Njeri Sahle

First Printing 2002

Cover Design: Roger Dormann
Cover Artwork: Mark Howes

Library of Congress Cataloging-in-Publication Data

The legacies of Julius Nyerere : influences on development discourse and practice in Africa / edited by David A. McDonald and Eunice Njeri Sahle.
p.cm. – (The politics of self-reliance / by Ngugi wa Thiong'o
– Julius Nyerere and the theory and practice of (un)democratic socialism in Africa / by John S. Saul – The challenge of development in Tanzania / by Julius E. Nyang'oro – The ethical foundation of Julius Nyerere's legacy / by Cranford Pratt – An economist's reflections on the legacies of Julius Nyerere / by Gerry Helleiner – Julius Nyerere's critical education thought / by Eunice Njeri Sahle – Inspiration for a new generation? / by David A. McDonald – Defining socialism in Tanzania / by Julius K. Nyerere.)
ISBN 0-86543-881 (hardback) – ISBN 0-86543-882-X (pbk.)
  1. Nyerere, Julius K. (Julius Kambarage), 1922–Influence. 2. Tanzania–Politics and government–1964- 3. Africa–Politics and government–1960- I. Mcdonald, David A. (David Alexander) II. Sahle, Eunice Njeri. III. Series.
DT448.25.N9 L44 2002
967.804'092–dc21

                                   2002001569

TABLE OF CONTENTS

v

About the Contributors

Gerry Helleiner was the first Director of the Economic Research Bureau at the University of Dar es Salaam from 1966 to 1968. During that time he was also a member of the Boards of Directors of the Bank of Tanzania and the Tanzania Sisal Corporation (after nationalization) and a member of the National Economic Council. He has acted as an advisor in Tanzania on many occasions, including his participation in the early 1980s as one of three advisors appointed jointly by the government of Tanzania and the World Bank to develop a Tanzanian stabilisation and adjustment programme after a breakdown in relations with the IMF.

David A. McDonald is Director of the Development Studies programme at Queen's University in Kingston. His research interests include development theory, political ecology, and urbanization, with a focus on South and Southern Africa.

Julius Nyang'oro is Chair of the Department of African and Afro-American Studies at the University of North Carolina at Chapel Hill. His has written extensively on issues pertaining to Africa's political economy and his books include: *Civil Society and Democratic Development in Africa* and *The State and Capitalist Development in Africa*.

Cranford Pratt was the first Principal of the University College, Dar es Salaam, from 1961 to 1965. He then revisited Tanzania recurrently until 1982 and wrote extensively at that time on Tanzanian politics and development issues, including *The Critical Phase in Tanzania, 1945 to1968: Nyerere and the Emergence of a Socialist Strategy*. He is an emeritus professor of political science at the University of Toronto.

Eunice Njeri Sahle is Assistant Professor in the Department of African and Afro-American Studies and International Studies at the University of North Carolina at Chapel Hill. Her research interests include the political economy of development, ethno-nationalism, international relations and Canadian foreign policy.

John S. Saul taught for the best part of a decade in Africa (Tanzania and Mozambique) and has written, co-written and edited some ten books on African political developments, including *Essays on the Political Economy of Africa, The Crisis in South Afarica, Socialist Ideology and the Struggle for Southern Africa, Recolonization and Resistance: Southern Africa in the 1990s* , and *Namibia's Liberation Struggle: The Two-Edged Sword*. He teaches at York University in Toronto.

Ngugi wa Thiong'o is a novelist and playwright who has written extensively on politics and language in east Africa. His novels have won international acclaim and include *The River Between, A Grain of Wheat, Petals of Blood*, and *Matigari*. He is currently the Erich Maria Remarque Professor in Languages at New York University

Biography

Julius K. Nyerere

April 13, 1922 - born in Butiama Village near Lake Victoria.

1934 - commenced primary school in Musoma (age of 12).

1936 - placed first on an entrance exam for Tabora Government Secondary School.

1943 - completed his secondary education.

1946 - obtained a Teacher's Diploma from Makerere University.

1946-1948 - teaching Biology and English at St. Mary's Secondary School, Tabora.

1948 - married Maria Magige, with whom he has 6 children over the years.

1952 - obtained a Master of Arts degree in History and Economics, University of Edinburgh.

1952 - elected president of Tanganyika African Association which he begins to transform from an elite social club into a mass political party.

1953 - began teaching History, English and Kiswahili, at St. Francis' College, near Dar es Salaam.

July 7, 1954 - founded and became first president of Tanganyika African National Union (TANU).

1954 - addressed the Trusteeship Council and Fourth Committee of the United Nations in New York on behalf of TANU.

1955 - compelled by the colonial authorities to choose between teaching and giving up his political activities, he resigns from St. Francis.

1958 - elected Member of the Legislative Assembly in the first parliamentary elections in which the African population had the franchise. Becomes the Leader of the Opposition (to the non-elected government).

September 1960 - becomes Chief Minister of the first Internal Government Administration of Tanganyika.

December 9, 1961 - becomes Prime Minister of the first Government of Independent Tanganyika.

January 23, 1962 - resigns as Prime Minister but continues as President of TANU.

December 1962 - becomes Tanganyika's first President after it becomes a Republic.

1964 - elected President of the Republic of Tanzania following the unification of Tanganyika and Zanzibar.

February 1967 – introduced Arusha Declaration marking a formal commitment to socialism and self-reliance.

1971 – introduced Leadership (*Mwongozo*) Code of conduct for bureaucrats and politicians.

1973-76 - villagization programme moved nearly 13 million rural farmers into 8000 villages.

1977 - founding member and Chairman of Chama Cha Mapinduzi (CCM), a new party formed by a merger of TANU and the Afro-Shiraz Party of Zanzibar.

1978-79 - launched war with Uganda.

1980-85 - unsuccessful negotiations with the International Monetary Fund.

1984 - became head of the Organization of African Unity.

November 5, 1985 - retired as president of Tanzania but continues as chairman of CCM.

1987-1990 - served as chairman of the South Commission.

1990 - retired as chairman of the CCM.

1990-99 - served as chair of the South Centre, successor of the South Commission.

1996 - founded the Mwalimu Nyerere Foundation.

April 1996 - served as chief mediator in the Burundi civil war.

October 14, 1999 - died of leukemia.

PUBLICATIONS

(1963) *William Shakespeare's Julius Caesar.* Nairobi: Oxford University Press [translation into Swahili verse also published as *Juliasi Kaizari.* Dar es Salaam: OUP, 1969].

(1966) *Freedom and Unity.* London: Oxford University Press.

(1966) with Joshua Nkomo, *Rhodesia: The Case for Majority Rule.* New Delhi: Indian Council for Africa.

(1967) *After the Arusha Declaration: The Presidential Address to the National Conference of Tanganyika African National Union, Mwanza, 16th October.* Dar Es Salaam: Ministry of Information and Tourism.

(1967) with D. Nichol and C. Pratt, *The Inaugural Lectures of the University of Zambia.* Manchester: Manchester University Press.

(1967) "Foreword," in K. Japhet and E. Seaton, *The Meru Land Case.* Nairobi: East African Publishing House.

(1968) *Uhuru na Ujamaa: Freedom and Socialism. A Selection from Writings & Speeches, 1965-1967.* London, NY and Dar es Salaam: Oxford University Press.

(1969). *Nyerere on Socialism.* London, NY and Dar es Salaam: Oxford University Press.

(1969). *Mapebari wa Venisi.* Dar es Salaam: Oxford University Press.

(1974) *Freedom & Development, Uhuru Na Maendele: A selection from writings and speeches 1968-1973.* London, NY and Dar es Salaam: Oxford University Press.

(1974) *Man and Development*. London, NY and Dar es Salaam: Oxford University Press.

(1974) "Education in Africa and Contemporary Tanzania," in *Education and Black Struggle: Notes from the Colonized World*, special issue of the Harvard Educational Review edited by the Institute of the Black World.

(1977) *Ujamaa - Essays on Socialism*, London, NY and Dar es Salaam: Oxford University Press.

(1977) "Introduction," in L. Stirling, *Tanzanian Doctor*. London: C. Hurst.

(1978) *Crusade for Liberation*, London, NY and Dar es Salaam: Oxford University Press.

(1978) "Development is for Man, by Man, and of Man: The Declaration of Dar es Salaam" in Budd L. Hall and J. Roby Kidd (eds.), *Adult Education: A design for action*, Oxford: Pergamon.

(1979) avec Samir Amin and Daniel Perron, *Le Dialog Inégal*. Genève: Tiers Monde.

(1980) "Foreword," in G.M. Carter and E.P. Morgan (eds.), *From the Frontline: Speeches of Sir Seretse Khama*. Stanford: Hoover University Press.

(1980) "Introduction," in M. Sears, *Years of High Promise: From Trusteeship to Nationhood*. Washington: American University Press.

(1985) "Education in Tanzania," *Harvard Educational Review* 55, no. 1.

(1987) *Reflections on Africa and its Future*. Lagos: Nigerian Institute of International Affairs.

(1988) "Foreword," in G.M. Houser, *No One Can Stop the Struggle: Glimpses of Africa's Liberation Struggle*. NY: Pilgrim Press.

(1989) "Foreword," in P. Johnson and D. Martin, *Frontline South Africa: Destructive Engagement*. NY: Four Walls, Eight Windows.

(1990) "Foreword," in C. Raghavan, *Recolonization: GATT, the Uruguay Round and the Third World*. London: Zed Press.

(1990) *The South Commission: The Challenge to the South*. NY and London: Oxford University Press.

(1992) "Foreword," in Olusegun Obasanjo and Felix Mosha (eds.), *Conference on Security, Stability, Development and Co-operation in Africa*. Abeokuta: African Leadership Forum.

(1993) "Foreword," in South Commission, *Facing the Challenge: Responses to the Report of the South Commission*. London: Zed Press.

(1993) "Reflections," in R. Sandbrook and Mohamed Halfani (eds.), *Empowering People*. Toronto: Centre for Urban and Community Studies.

(1993) *Tanzania! Tanzania!* Dar es Salaam: Tanzania Publishing House [a collection of poems in Swahili].

(1993) *Uongozi Wetu na Hatima ya Tanzania*. Harare: Zimbabwe Publishing House.

(1994) *Africa's Development in Global Perspective*. Bellville: EFSA Institute for Theological Studies.

(1995) *Our Leadership and the Destiny of Tanzania*. Harare: African Publishing Group.

(1997) *Africa Today and Tomorrow*. Dar es Salaam: Mwalimu Nyerere Foundation.

(1997) *Africa: The Third Liberation*. Edinburgh: Centre of African Studies.

(1999) "Foreword," in R. Sadleir, *Tanzania's Journey to Republic*. NY: Radcliffe.

(2000) "Foreword," in Yoweri Museveni, *What is Africa's Problem?* Minneapolis: University of Minnesota Press.

PREFACE

When Julius Kambarage Nyerere died in October 1999 there was a remarkable outpouring of sympathy and remembrance from around the world. Critics and admirers alike wrote glowing tributes about his role in African and global politics and attempted to assess the legacies that he had left behind.

For those of us in North America who were unable to attend the funeral there was a strong desire to gather and talk about the man who was president of Tanzania for more than 20 years and whose mark on that country, and the African continent more broadly, will last much longer.

The essays in this volume stem from just such a gathering: a conference held at Queen's University, Canada, in February of 2000 entitled *The Legacies of Julius Nyerere: Influences on Development Discourse and Practice in Africa*. The fact that the conference was held in the clutch of a cold Canadian winter and still managed to attract close to 200 participants from Canada and the United States, speaks both to the enormous influence that Nyerere has on popular and scholarly work on Africa as well as the obvious need that people felt to talk and commiserate about his death.

But the conference was not merely an uncritical celebration of Nyerere's life. Nor would Nyerere have wanted it that way. The purpose of the conference was to discuss Nyerere's policies and philosophies and to reflect critically on his influences on development discourse and practice in Tanzania and Africa – good, bad and undecided. The essays and commentaries provided here are intended as a contribution to this debate.

The first five chapters of the collection are based on panel presentations made at the conference by scholars and authors who had either known and worked with Nyerere, been closely involved in the development debates in Tanzania, and/or had themselves grown up in Tanzania under Nyerere's political tenure. The presentations are reproduced here in the order that they were given and are intended to provide readers with the presenters' personal reflections on Nyerere's life and legacies.

Author Ngugi wa Thiong'o writes in Chapter One about Nyerere's life-long commitment to African languages and how this legacy ties into a recent conference on African languages and literatures in Asmara, Eritrea. In Chapter Two, scholar-activist John Saul talks about Nyerere's mixed record on democratic practice while in Chapter Three Julius Nyang'oro discusses some of the more contemporary challenges facing Tanzania and how these link with Nyerere's policies and ideas. In Chapters Four and Five former policy advisors to Nyerere – Cranford Pratt and Gerry Helleiner – reflect on the ethical foundations of Nyerere's policies and his economic record, respectively.

Chapter Six is a transcription of the question and answer period that took place after the formal presentations and includes a summary analysis by Colin Leys. In some respects this was the richest part of the conference because of the wealth of experience and knowledge in the audience and the subsequent opportunity for panellists to respond to questions and comments.

Chapters Seven and Eight are contributions from the editors of this volume (and organizers of the conference). Eunice Njeri Sahle's chapter explores Nyerere's ideas on the role of education in Tanzania's development and its relevance to development discourse and socialist practice more generally. David McDonald's chapter looks south to the new centre of political gravity on the continent – South Africa – and asks if the political leadership in that country is as "inspiring" as Nyerere's was in Tanzania.

Lastly, there is an Appendix which is a reproduction of the introduction to Nyerere's 1968 book *"Uhuru na Ujamaa: Freedom and Socialism"* (by kind permission of Masoud Nassor Masoud, Editor of Oxford University Press, Tanzania). This essay provides an overview of Nyerere's vision of socialism and is intended, in his own words, to "enlarge upon the socialist goal which Tanzania has accepted as its objective, and upon the manner in which Tanzania can progress towards this goal." The paper is reproduced here for several reasons. First, it demonstrates the incredibly articulate and alive manner in which Nyerere spoke and wrote and is an eloquent example of his formidable writing style. Second, the paper provides an intellectually rigorous description of what socialism means in an African context. It is non-dogmatic in its allowance for different versions of social, political and economic life under the banner of "socialism" while at the same time insisting on a core set of moral values and material rights. In this sense, Nyerere's essay is still very contemporary and reminds us, in this era of global neoliberal hegemony, that a more just and equitable vision of the world is still possible. Whether we use the term socialism or not, Nyerere's description of the possibilities (and the challenges) of a post-capitalist world are as exciting today as they were more than 30 years ago.

We would like to thank everyone who participated in the conference in order to make it such a success, especially those who contributed papers, questions and commentary. We would also like to thank Gisèle Morin-Labatut and Rohinton Medora of the International Development Research Centre (IDRC) for their support for this initiative and the IDRC itself for helping to fund the conference and publication. Thanks also to Kassahun Checole from Africa World Press for his keen interest in the project. Christina Decarie provided invaluable assistance with administrative support, Meg Freer provided careful copyediting and Agnes Appusigah assisted with the organization of the conference. Marc Epprecht prepared the short biography of Nyerere's life. Mark Howes did layout and design for the text and cover.

The conference was organized under the auspices of the Studies in National and International Development (SNID) programme at Queen's.

We dedicate the book to the memory of Julius Kambarage Nyerere.

CHAPTER ONE

The Politics of Self-Reliance:

JULIUS NYERERE AND THE ASMARA DECLARATION

Ngugi wa Thiong'o

There is a way in which Nyerere comes to all of us, both in a personal sense and in a collective sense. I think every African person, even if they have never read Nyerere, would appreciate the example he gave to Africa. The fact, for example, that an African president, a leader, could peacefully leave office and still live in the same country was a tremendous contribution, especially when seen against the prevailing context of the time in which many leaders died in office or were gunned out of office. That sense of orderly succession is a tremendous example of Nyerere's moral leadership, reflected in his own personal life and in much of his writings.

This moral leadership, incidentally, is also reflected in the leadership of Eritrea today, which, by way of introduction, brings me to the subject matter of this chapter: the Asmara Declaration and how it relates to the legacy of Julius Nyerere.

The Declaration is the outcome of a conference entitled Against All Odds: African Languages and Literatures into the 21st Century, held in January of 2000 in Asmara, Eritrea. The conference brought together writers organised around three sectors. The first sector was writers from different parts of the continent who wrote in African languages. It was the first time that a gathering of African writers whose primary communication was African languages had ever taken place on African soil and involved writers from Southern Africa, East Africa, West Africa and North Africa. The second group of participants was publishers who were interested in publishing in African languages or who have at one point or other published or expressed an interest in publishing in African languages. The third sector was scholars from inside and outside Africa interested in this issue of African languages and their relationship to the development of Africa. It was, in a way, a very unique conference because it brought so many elements together. Perhaps ten years from now we shall be talking about the intellectual development of Africa in terms of pre-Asmara and post-Asmara positions! Personally, as an African and as a writer, the conference was one of the most enjoyable and intellectually satisfying of my life.

I began writing novels, short stories, plays and essays in 1960 when I was a student of English at Makerere University in Uganda, which was then an affiliate of London University. I have therefore been wielding a pen for at least 40 years — more than half my life — because I was born in 1938. From 1960 to 1977, I wrote in English, even though my books were mostly about Kenya and Kenyan people. From 1977 to the present, I have written all of my novels, short stories, plays and books for children in Gikuyu, one of the more than thirty African languages in Kenya. Thus, half of my writing life has been taken up with English and the other half with Gikuyu.

During that 40-year period, I have been invited to many conferences on African writing in English, starting with the famous one in 1963 called A Conference of Writers with English Expression held in Makerere. With the exception of the Asmara conference, and one at the School of African Studies in London, I have never been invited to, or even heard about, a conference dedicated to discussing literature in African languages, or a conference of writers who write in African languages. I may stand to be corrected, but this means that since the early 1960s, when African countries started getting their independence, non-African languages have been the ones setting the terms of debate on the literature on the continent. In schools and colleges in Africa and abroad, literature, which is taught under the label of "African literature", is still that which is written mostly in non-African languages (i.e., English, French, Portuguese, etc.).

Previously, conferences to which I was invited were about African literature yet they never took seriously writers working in African languages. The trend of these conferences has historically been to glorify those writing in other languages. In general, a writer in any one African country could have been writing solely in an African language for any number of years, without ever being heard outside the country. But let another person in the same country write and publish just one novel in English, French, or Portuguese, and he or she begins to receive invitations to numerous conferences on African literature, both within Africa and outside Africa. Soon that person becomes the representative of literature from that country and their books may become canonised by entering school curriculum. This has led to the aforementioned phenomenon of non-African languages determining who is an African writer and who writes for Africa.

The situation of European and African languages, vis-à-vis the continent, reminds me of a story I first read in Kenya. The story is called The Gentleman of the Jungle, which is a variation of another story, The Arab and the Comrade, I believe. You may know the story, I am sure. I will summarise it here very briefly. The Gentleman of the Jungle is the lion. One day a man is seated, relaxing inside his house. The lion is outside the house and starts begging the man to let him inside. The lion says: "It is so cold outside here, can I just let my head in the house." Of course, the man allows first the head into the house, then the shoulders, front legs, and when the lion is in completely, it says to the man: "There is not room enough for you and me in this house — Get out!" So in the end, the man, who is the owner of the house, is outside and the lion is in. It is interesting because it is the lion who determines the history of the house once inside. Thus, different languages have become like that lion and they often take the space that was occupied by African languages. They own the homestead, otherwise called African literature.

As mentioned earlier, the Asmara conference was the first conference on African soil to bring together in one place African writers and world scholars to discuss the state of scholarship on African literature and knowledge in African languages. But rather than meeting as Francophones or Anglophones we were meeting as Afriphones. But the conference was a watershed in Africa's intellectual history in other ways as well. First, during the conference I realised that we had not really gone there to argue whether we should be writing in African languages. This is an argument that I have been having with people from all over the world, but at this conference it was assumed that we should be. Second, we had not gone there to argue whether African languages have adequate vocabularies or not, another argument that I have been encountering for the last twenty years. Third, we had not gone there to argue how we could best sing with other people's voices, while still trying to retain our own identities, which again is an argument you find over and over again. Both scholars and writers say that we can use the language and make it our own. In essence, we were in Asmara in tune with the spirit of the saying "borrowed jewelry tires the wearer."

To illustrate this I will tell a short story that I find quite interesting about borrowed jewelry. Two friends, young men, were going to a dance. Let us call one John and the other one James. James and John are preparing themselves to go to this dance. They are putting on their best clothes, especially since they have been told that the ladies who are there have come from all the way from another city. In fact, there are people from all over the country gathered at the dance. They are from all over Canada and are all gathered in Kingston. They have to look their best. James turns around and tells John that the suit he is wearing is terrible. How can he go to the dance without a tie and a three-piece suit? John agrees, saying he cannot attend such an important dance without a suit and tie. John then asks James if he can borrow one of his suits. James lends his friend one of his suits. Once John wears the suit he becomes very happy because it fits him even better than it fits James.

When they arrive at the party, all the ladies want to dance with John. He dances so much that at one point he has to loosen his tie because he is so hot. James then makes a beeline towards him and says: "You know, the suit that I lent you looks awful if you wear the tie loose. Can you please tighten it a little?" This embarrasses John so much that he goes to another part of the party to avoid his friend. It is very embarrassing to be reminded that the clothes do not actually belong to him. After that, everything seems to be fine until finally they go to dinner. While coffee is being served after dinner James tells John: "Hey, my friend, be very careful with that coffee. Don't spill coffee on the suit which I lent you."

There is a similar tendency when African people use English and French. They are always reminded in one way or another that the language is not really theirs, even when they are using it very, very well. There are always hints and guesses as to how they came to learn English so well, how accessible their accents are, and so on: "So-and-so is such a good writer. The way he uses our language is even better than native speakers themselves." For me then, the week in Asmara will be marked on the calendar as the time when African languages, from the different parts of the continent, came together to reassert their political right to being the spoken tongues of Africa, and hence claimed their homestead.

Significantly, Nyerere was at the center of this conference in many ways. First, when the conference was being organised, I knew the organisers were thinking of Nyerere as being a key moderator. They really wanted him to be at the conference. By the time they were sending out flyers, however, he become seriously ill. Although he died before the conference was held, his presence was felt throughout the conference. On the fourth day of the program, for example, we had an evening for Nyerere and the event was overwhelmingly attended. It was a very large hall and it was completely packed. Again, in the presence of writers from different parts of the world, we had performances or statements from different parts of Africa and the world, talking about Nyerere.

Why did people feel his presence at that conference on the future of African languages in scholarships and literature? I want to try to explore this question in terms of the concepts of home and homecoming, or in another sense, returning to one's source or to the root or to the base. To think of returning to the base in Africa we have to always remember that the continent in both its positive and negative aspects is a product of colonialism and the travails of African people against it. These two forces should never be forgotten. They are linked together; it is not one or the other, it is both. Colonialism was essentially a process of taking over a people's homestead and of taking people away from their collective way. The concept of the home is very important. The homestead is a person's base, and colonialism can be seen as a process of alienating people from their total environment. That is their base and their way of life. The environment could be economic, political and cultural. The coloniser for obvious reasons did not bring lands into Africa, nor did he bring labour. He seized the lands and then grew coffee, tea and mined precious metals with the labour of those whose land he had already taken. When these raw materials were processed in Europe, they became available to Africa at mostly high prices.

What about the continent's political environment? The coloniser, again, did not bring armies from Europe. In most cases, he made armies out of the divisions between African peoples and he helped set community against community, region against region, and clan against clan. They all ended up being alienated from their power base while the coloniser became empowered over all the spheres of the local community. In other words, the coloniser used power to get power and then used this power against the colonised community as a whole.

Now, in my view, one of the most serious results of this colonial process was the alienation of African people from the cultural environment. The cultural environment is what carries people's way into the world, just as we have the home, and every morning you set out on a path that links you to different parts of the country, the town, the environment, etc. In a symbolic sense then, the cultural environment is what carries people's way into the world. This is what tells people who they are and leads people into their collective homestead.

To alienate people from their cultural way is to deprive people of the power to connect with the world and their base. Unless you know where you are from it is almost impossible to know where you are going next. In other words, if an individual loses the sense of the way to his or her homestead it is very difficult to know how to connect with anything around them.

Language is our way to the world, so to speak. The quickest means of achieving the alienation of a people from their way and from their power base is surely through language. Here, we see language as part of a naming system. To process the world, we have to name the world. It is by naming the world that we differentiate a, b and c. Thus, if you talk about the first signal to the world, it is a naming system. When I hear the world Ngugi, I respond to the sound called Ngugi. To me, that sound Ngugi represents a specific sound system. James, which is a name I used to be called, represents a different sound system, one that points to a different type of inheritance whether I like it or not. It has nothing to do with what I may think in the abstract. When I was James Ngugi, James was pointing to one inheritance and Ngugi was pointing to another. In this respect James was qualifying Ngugi. I was Ngugi who was qualified by James. James authenticated my being.

Historically, ruling classes have utilised language in efforts to alienate people from their homesteads. A few examples will suffice here. In eighteenth-century America, a certain slave owner in Virginia, William Lynch, wrote to fellow slave owners on how to break the resistance of the slaves. It was interesting how he quickly zeroed in on language as the most effective way of linking the mind and the body of the enslaved. I quote him: "We must completely annihilate the mother tongue of the nigger and make him a new mule. We must institute a new language that involves their new lives and work." He is saying that you create a mule out of a "nigger" through language. The loss of language would inevitably lead to a loss of any connections with one's own history and worldviews. Again, we go back to William Lynch. He says: "The mind has a strong drive to correct and re-correct itself over a period of time, if it can touch some substantial, original historical basis and the best way to deal with this phenomenon is to shave off the roots bent by history and create a multiplicity of phenomenon of illusions." A very apt phrase, this one: "multiplicity of illusions". It becomes terrible when we use illusions as reality, but this was exactly what the slave owners intended.

Let me give you other examples. This one is from India. A Mr. McCauley — Secretary of Education, a member of Supreme Council and someone who was involved in devising educational policy for India in the nineteenth century during British colonial rule — viewed the introduction of English in India's education system as a means of creating a class of natives Indian in colour but with an English mind. This would result in the creation of a class that was a sort of bastion between the colonising minority and the colonised majority.

In Kenya, where I come from, in 1954 when we were on the verge of the Mau Mau struggle against the British colonial presence there was a change of language policy. Previously, the colonial regime had discouraged Africans from learning English because it feared that this would lead them to accessing alternative ideas and challenging the colonial project. In 1954, however, there was a significant change. The then-colonial governor, Mitchell, using words almost identical to those used by McCauley in India in 1834, declared that henceforth the government would encourage the expansion of the English language so as to facilitate the emergence of a literate African class. Here the parallel with the Indian case is obvious since this class in Kenya would result in the emergence of an African middle class with an English mind-set and standards.

In all three cases the colonisers are all talking about lynching the mind of the enslaved so as to create a "multiplicity of illusions" (even about their own bodies and environment). Alienation from one's environment brings the disease that we could call 'not knowing oneself'. When you don't know yourself, you don't know what happens. There is a tragic story of a Kenyan lady who went to the United States, got a little confused over the years, and one day was stopped at one of the airports completely naked, saying she was going home. During her stay she became confused, not knowing herself, not knowing the results generated by a crisis of identity and the actions that she could actually take to return to her base, her homestead. Those who do not know themselves are like persons drugged. They can be turned anyway, without any resistance. In some ways, William Lynch, the slave owner, says that quite clearly.

Viewed in historical terms, we could argue that the struggle for independence in Africa was a struggle about control of the continent's entire environment by African people. In my view, Nyerere, more than anybody else, understood this the sense of returning to one's homestead or being in control of the entirety of a people's environment. This was particularly evidenced by his emphasis of the idea of self-reliance. And self-reliance, understood in its totality, does not mean alienation or isolation from the rest of the world. Its basic underlining is a sense of the base, the return to the base, being sure of your base and then connecting with the rest of the world. This seems to me what underlies all the programs that he came up with. The success or failure of any particular program does not matter; what is important is the sense that self-reliance has to do with interconnection with the base and starting from that base. It really means reclamation of the economic, political and cultural base of the process of development.

In this case, Nyerere's attitude to language and to Swahili becomes very pivotal. In fact, in understanding this later development in his thought, it is interesting to note that he starts with translating Shakespeare into Swahili thus showing, with that one stroke, what we have been discussing all along: the question of getting knowledge from outside and making it available to the local linguistic base. Obviously, as a leader, he did more than that, because from a language point of view, he gave Swahili a home and a regional base.

However, in most other African countries we all know that something went wrong at the raising of the flag. By the time we came to raise the flag we found that the mind of the elite had already been lynched. They had lost their way to the homestead and they became like those talked of in the Bible: having ears but not being able to hear; having eyes but not being able to see. It is the same as a multiplicity of illusions. They have eyes, although they are not actually seeing, but they think they are seeing.

I would like to give a few examples to illustrate the blindness of those who have eyes and cannot see and the deafness of those who have ears and cannot hear because of the multiplicity of illusions planted in their minds by the likes of colonial William Lynch. I give you these examples because they affect all of us from the African continent. There is not a single African who is not affected by the situation in which we find ourselves in the world today. Africa is one of the richest continents in the world in terms of minerals. There is not a single mineral resource that cannot be found in Africa. But Africa is the poorest continent in the world. The Democratic Republic of Congo (DRC), which produces minerals that help the most advanced countries to go the moon and other places, itself has barely any roads!

Another example is in the realm of education. African countries spend a sizeable percentage of their national incomes on education, but the knowledge generated generally ends up hidden in different languages. To me, if there is any tragedy about Africa, it is precisely that. There are universities in Africa, colleges, and money — up to 80% of our budgets — producing all these minds with the hope that they get knowledge and put that knowledge to use. Given Africa's historical developments and its place in the international system only a few of its people get access to education. Thus in most of the education systems on the continent the idea is always that those who are fortunate enough to be educated should return to the base, the homestead. What do we do instead? We get to a place that is comfortable for ourselves and forget about the rest.

We are all basically in that kind of situation, all of us collectively in Africa, because when we arrive at the other end of the education process we forget about our homestead. We are comfortable within the linguistic home of English or French and forget those at the base. In our comfortable zone, we start declaring that the best thing for those people is to come here. We keep saying: "If only they could find their way here." We keep saying English, English. So, the question that I keep asking, and the one I think the Asmara conference was very cognizant of, is this: If 100% of the knowledge generated in Africa ends up in different languages, and yet it is the majority of African people who most need this knowledge, why can't we put all that knowledge into African languages instead of the current practice of hiding it in different languages?

How do we deal with the ethnic divisions? It is true that in each African country there are many nationalities that speak different languages. While the situation is complex, my view is that we should not hide our heads in the sand like the ostrich and pretend that this is not so, or that we can solve the problems of that reality by importing a language of national salvation from Europe. We all need to remember that there was a time when humans used to think of seas, oceans, gravity and space as barriers, enemies of the people, until they learned how to use them. Without our understanding of gravity, we would not be flying today. What seemed to be a barrier at one point turned to a positive development when a different set of questions was posed. Consequently, what we need to do is to pose a different question in Africa as far as language and ethnicity, are concerned, not to wish away the multiplicity of those languages or ethnicity because that is the reality we start with. The question we should start asking is: How could the many languages be utilised to bring about the unity of African peoples within a country and then within Africa as a whole?

If you look at Africa in terms of the notion of shared communities a different picture emerges. For instance, in Kenya, there are Masai people on the Kenyan side and Masai people on the Tanzanian side. So, if we were to find a natural or ethnic basis of unity for Tanzania and Kenya we do not have to go far from the reality of our situation. We have a shared community already, one we care about. In Northern Kenya and Southern Ethiopia we find another shared community comprising the Oromo people. In the context of Kenya and Somalia there are Somali people in both countries. Kenya and Sudan also share common communities. Eritrea and Ethiopia also have shared communities. The list goes on.

If you look at Africa this way you see a very different picture. What you see are links in the chain of unity. We think of shared communities as when you form a circle and link hands. We become the links of chain, from South Africa all the way to Morocco or Egypt. My point is that if we pose a different question, we can turn our languages and shared communities into a positive force.

A first step in this direction might mean developing literatures and knowledge in African languages and encouraging the translation of literary works into the different African languages. Although I still write in Gikuyu, my work could be translated into Tigrinya, Swahili or Ibo, Yoruba, Chichewa, and Zulu, and the other way around. Then the children of different nationalities could read and identify with the stories, characters and names set in a different region. In time, a child from one nationality may come to feel that he knows the characters and names of a different nationality almost as well as those of his immediate neighbourhood. This also creates respect for other languages and cultures and produces wonderful stories and situations. In time, children from one country would find that their languages share a common culture and heritage. The same would obviously be true of the continent as a whole. This would create a good, solid, cultural foundation for specific countries and for Africa. Translations and the learning of more than one African language would be built into the school and university curriculum.

In many ways the meeting in Eritrea was a first step towards such a development. It was also a celebration of the fact that, despite all these odds, African languages have actually existed in literature or writing for centuries, and a challenge to scholars to create literatures and knowledge which speak to the most urgent needs of our people, for economic and political survival. One of the ways this can be done is through a collective effort and alliances with our own countries. What we need for African countries is an alliance with the various governments, writers and publishers. We have to have governments that establish correct democratic policies. It is impossible to introduce effective language policies in Africa when we get governments with colonised, lynched mentalities. This is the very mentality that you see at work in Africa today, where African people do not feel any sense of shame or embarrassment about hacking the noses off their enemies. Even when there are wars there are rules governing how you treat enemies. Now, we have a situation in Africa where if I get my enemy I have no problem in cutting off his nose, his ears, his arms: do the most degrading thing possible to a fellow African in front of television cameras. In the creation of a decolonised mentality we need all those alliances of governments, publishers, and scholars in Africa and also scholars outside Africa. The establishment of innovative language policies will be an important step in our struggle to rebuild Africa's homesteads and connection with the rest of the world.

In my view, development of African languages should not mean isolation from other languages of the world. There is a lot that African languages can learn from those of Europe, Asia and Latin America. African languages must be open to the heritage of those Africans who have now built new nations and communities in the Caribbean, the Americas, the Pacific and so on. Africans who have made their homes in these new lands also have to be challenged to connect with Africa through a knowledge of other languages in addition to those they actually now normally use. In other words, without abandoning it, they can use as a base the standard language of their new country in the Caribbean, America, the Pacific, but they can connect to Africa through another African language. I would like to challenge writers and intellectuals of African descent wherever they are to do for African languages what intellectuals have done for other languages, i.e., to produce the best that can be written and thought in their own languages.

I would like to end by reading the Asmara declaration that came from the aforementioned conference, because in so many ways it brings together all the issues that I have been talking about, but in a very specific manner. The Asmara declaration is very important, because it is asking African scholars to take responsibility for their continent. They can no longer shy away from taking that responsibility and the challenge of being spokespeople for their continent. The declaration says:

That scholars from all regions of Africa convened in Asmara, Eritrea from 2 January to 15 January the year 2000 in a conference titled Against All Odds: African Languages and Literatures into the 21st Century. This is the first conference on African Languages and Literatures ever to be held on African soil with participants from East, West, North and Southern Africa and from the Diaspora and by writers and scholars from around the world. We examined the state of African languages in literature, scholarship, publishing, education and administration in Africa and throughout the world. We celebrated the vitality of African languages and literatures and found their potential. We noted, with pride, that despite all the odds against them, African languages as vehicles of communication and knowledge survived for thousands of years. Colonialism created some of the most serious obstacles against African languages and literatures. We noted, with concern, the fact that these colonial obstacles still haunt independent Africa and continue to block the mind of the continent. We identified a profound incongruity in colonial languages speaking for the continent. At the start of a new century and millennium, Africa must firmly reject this incongruity and affirm a new beginning by turning to languages and heritage.

At this historical conference, we, writers and scholars from all regions of Africa gathered in Asmara, Eritrea declare that:

1) African languages must take on the duty, responsibility and the challenge of speaking for the continent.

2) The vitality and quality of African languages must be recognised as the basis for the future empowerment of African peoples.

3) The diversity of African languages reflects the rich cultural heritage of Africa and must be used as an instrument of African unity.

4) Dialogue among African languages is essential. African languages must use an instrument of translation to advance communication among all people, including the disabled.

5) African children have the right to attend school and learn in their mother tongue. Every effort should be made to develop African languages at all levels of education.

6) Promoting research on African languages is vital for the development or the advancement of African research and documentation would best be served by the use of African languages.

7) The effective and rapid development of science and technology in Africa depends on the use of African languages and modern technology must be used for the development of African languages.

8) Democracy is essential for the equal development of African languages and African languages are vital for the development of democracy based on equality and social justice.

9) African languages, like all languages, contain gender bias. The role of African languages in development must overcome this gender bias and achieve gender equality.

10) African languages are essential for the decolonisation of African minds and for the African renaissance. We hope this initiative that is set up based in Eritrea will be continued by annual conferences in different parts of Africa. In order to organise future conferences in different parts of Africa, to create a forum of dialogue, cooperation and politisation, a permanent secretariat will be established which will be initially based in Asmara, Eritrea. By listening to as many African languages as possible, on the basis of these principles, the Asmara declaration is affirmed by all participants in the conference. We call upon all African states, the Organization of African Unity, the United Nations and other international organisations that serve Africa to join this effort of recognition and support for African languages, with this declaration as a new basis for new policies and outlook.

We acknowledge with pride the retention of African languages in some parts of Africa and the Diaspora and the role of African languages in the formation of new languages, particularly in the Americas and the Caribbean. We urge all people in Africa and the Diaspora to join in the spirit of this declaration and become part of the efforts to realise its goals.

This was proclaimed in Asmara on 17 January 2000.

The Asmara declaration is a challenge collectively to each and every African scholar. Only we can actually set the path and it is not going to be easy because of the multiplicity of illusions we have had. However, the Asmara conference offers a new beginning. There was a sense for those attending the conference that they were embarking on a different intellectual course of action. For example, a Kenyan scholar at Cornell University presented a paper on environmental politics which he had written in his core language. At the end of the conference, he stood up and said: "I am going back to Cornell University, and I am going to write my Master's dissertation in the Gikuyu language." That was a challenge he set for himself right there in Asmara and he got a standing ovation. This is the kind of spirit I am talking about.

Chapter Two

Julius Nyerere and the Theory and Practice of (Un)Democratic Socialism in Africa

John S. Saul

For purposes of argument I would suggest that the career of Julius Nyerere as public actor can best be evaluated on three fronts: as a nationalist, a socialist and a democrat, although, as we will see, these three strands of his theory and practice cannot be readily disentangled.

I will say least about Nyerere as a nationalist, although it is perhaps too easy to forget that dimension of his undertakings, so much has happened since to the original project of anti-colonial and anti-racist nationalism in Africa. But let us remember that Nyerere was a key player in that first generation of successful African nationalist leaders who, in the postwar period refused to accept the refusal of the likes of Winston Churchill, that quintessential Colonel Blimp, to "preside over the dissolution of the British Empire." Let us also recall how seriously Nyerere took the "unfinished business" of Southern Africa, placing Tanzania squarely in the middle of the thirty-years war for Southern African liberation, as essential rear-base for many liberation movements and as the most active of protagonists of such essential Pan-African initiatives for liberation as PAFMECSA and, subsequently, the Organization of African Unity Liberation Committee.

As suggested, the nationalist moment in postcolonial Africa tends now to be consigned to the back pages of the history books. No doubt this is in part the case because its denouement, as prophetically foreseen by Frantz Fanon, was to prove so lacking in purpose and promise for the vast mass of Africans ostensibly liberated under its banner; this has proven to be as true for Southern Africa, including, most notably and most dispiritingly, South Africa, as it has been for Africa north of the Zambezi. Where Nyerere saw further than most, however, was in the fact that he complemented his nationalism — and this is my second point — with his own version of a socialist analysis and a socialist vision.

In saying this I tend, up to a point, to discount Nyerere's own professions that he was not so much realising socialism in Africa as he was realising "African Socialism": "Socialism...is an attitude of mind," he famously asserted. "We in Africa have no need of being 'converted' to socialism...[it is] rooted in our own past — in the traditional society which produced us."

When he is speaking in this way, it might almost be possible to now view Nyerere as addressing himself to a post-modern audience, honouring the integrity of indigenous culture against the pull of more Eurocentric leftist formulations. And yet this whole "African Socialism" discourse, so often associated with Nyerere (and others, like Senghor), seems to me too vague, even flaccid, in its practical implications and, in any case, for Nyerere, to be rather less central to his thought, in the long run, than the (relatively) hard-nosed analysis that actually came to provide the underpinnings for his own socialist practice. For Nyerere's overall project was actually, in the end, quite modernist and developmental (not swear words in my vocabulary, incidentally, but words that nonetheless flag ambiguities to which I will return). More important to note at this point in the argument is the fact that, in consequence, his analysis of the realities of actually-existing Africa proved to be at least as much Fanonist as Senghoriste, if not more so.

Take, for example, Nyerere's observations as to the nature of the new class already all too visible across the continent in its rush to power and in its naked self-interest. Of his many statements on this issue, a speech I myself heard him give in 1967 in Dar es Salaam (as summarised in *The Nationalist* newspaper) captures particularly clearly the issue at stake:

President Nyerere has called on the people of Tanzania to have great confidence in themselves and safeguard the nation's hard-won freedom. He has warned the people against pinning their hopes on the leadership who are apt to sell the people's freedom to meet their lusts. Mwalimu (Nyerere) warned that the people should not allow their freedom to be pawned as most of the leaders were purchasable. He warned further that in running the affairs of the nation the people should not look on their leaders as 'saints or prophets'. The President stated that the attainment of freedom in many cases resulted merely in the change of colours, white to black faces without ending exploitation and injustices, and above all without the betterment of the life of the masses. He said that while struggling for freedom the objective was clear but it was another thing when you have to remove your own people from the position of exploiters.

Or, as he added in another 1967 speech: "African leaders have their price these days. The moment one becomes a minister, his price also gets determined. The prices are not even big; some are bought for only 500, or a simple house."

Or take his statement in *Education for Self-Reliance* as to the likely impact of an untransformed education system on such processes of class formation:

The educational system introduced into Tanzania by the colonialists was modeled on the British system, but with an even heavier emphasis on subservient attitudes and on white-collar skills. Inevitably, too, it was based on the assumptions of a colonialist and capitalist society. It emphasised and encouraged the individualistic instincts of mankind, instead of his cooperative instincts. It led to the possession of individual material wealth being the major criterion of social merit and worth. This meant that colonial education induced attitudes of human inequality, and in practice underpinned the domination of the weak by the strong, especially in the economic field. [1]

Other punchy and provocative statements about the potential costs of class formation are to be found in abundance in such writings as *Socialism and Rural Development*.

There is, however, a second dimension of his move to complement nationalism with socialism that is of at least equal importance, one that marks the interpenetration of these two projects even more overtly. Here a particularly pungent formulation is one to be found in his essay, "Economic Nationalism":[2]

The question is not whether nations control their economy, but how they do so. The real ideological choice is between controlling the economy through domestic private enterprise or doing so through some state or collective institution.

But although this is an ideological choice, it is extremely doubtful whether it is a practical choice for an African nationalist. The pragmatist in Africa...will find that the choice is a different one. He will find that the choice is between foreign private ownership on the one hand, and local collective ownership on the other. For I do not think that there is a free state in Africa where there is sufficient local capital, or a sufficient number of local entrepreneurs, for locally based capitalism to dominate the economy. Private investment in Africa means overwhelming foreign private investment. A capitalist economy means a foreign-dominated economy. These are the facts of the African situation. The only way in which national control of the economy can be achieved is through the economic institution of socialism.

Moreover, as Nyerere completed his argument:

To Tanzanians this inevitable choice is not unwelcome. We are committed to the creation of a classless society in which every able-bodied citizen is contributing to the economy through work, and we believe that this can only be obtained when the major means of production are publicly owned and controlled. But the fact remains that our recent socialist measures were not taken out of blind adherence to dogma. They are intended to serve the society.

"To serve the society." A moral imperative, then, but also a necessary development strategy; it is all the more relevant now if Colin Leys and I are right to think, as we have argued in a recent essay, that what we now see is the further "relegation [of Africa] to the margins of the global economy, with no visible prospect for continental development along capitalist lines" and that the crucial bottom-line of African renewal must therefore be a "renewed socialist thrust". As for Tanzanian socialism itself, debate will continue as to whether, on the one hand, lack of clarity in its self-definition and lack of subtlety in its practice were most responsible for undermining its prospects, or whether, on the other hand, such a project had little chance of success in any case under the conditions global capitalism offered Africa at the time (or even now). Still, whether we agree or not with Cran Pratt's position (in an eloquent obituary published in *Southern Africa Report*) regarding Nyerere's socialist programme — that "Few would now claim that many of these [the reference is to Nyerere's socialist policy measures] were appropriate instruments for the development of a poor country, especially one whose public service was already overextended" (I do not agree, as it happens) — it is difficult to quarrel with the correctness of Nyerere's basic premise that the global capitalist system did not, does not, serve Africa well.

It is a theme he returned to over and over again both while he was still president of Tanzania and equally vigorously after he had stepped down from that position and continued to play the role of international gadfly on development issues, as for example when he once sought to strike back at the strictures of structural adjustment, with the charge that the IMF has an ideology of economic and social development which it is trying to impose on poor countries irrespective of their own clearly stated policies. And when we reject IMF conditions, we hear the threatening whisper: "Without accepting our condition, you will not get our money, and you will get no other money." Indeed, we have already heard hints from some quarters that money or credit will not be made available to us until we have reached an understanding with the IMF. When did the IMF become an International Ministry of Finance? When did nations agree to surrender to it their power of decision-making?

Here is the "Spirit of Seattle" well *avant la lettre* surely, a spirit of proto-socialist critique that, interestingly enough, also continues to inspire Nyerere's daughter who, only a month after her father's death, was to be found speaking at a Jubilee 2000 workshop in Johannesburg and invoking, as part of an ongoing struggle against the African debt, her father's attack of the early 1980s upon what he then called the "international debt cartel". It is the emphases and actions Ms. Nyerere was here invoking that, I would argue, make Nyerere's writings so important a resource for a new generation of Africans like his daughter, as they reactivate their struggle for social, political and economic transformation along, dare I predict it, socialist lines.

But what, finally, of Nyerere as democrat? Much has been written of Nyerere's political and constitutional innovations, and indeed, Cran Pratt, in his obituary, seems prepared to grant Nyerere far higher marks on this front than for his socialist endeavours. And yet, in my judgementand in the long run, it is in the political realm that the most dramatic flaws in Nyerere's progressive practice are to be found.

There is a problem here. I have used the phrase "Nyerere's socialism" — and we speak of "Nyerere's political initiatives" — as if these were relatively unproblematic formulations. But such undertakings were refracted through the real world of

Tanzania's nationalist politics. Even Nyerere could not make policy just as he wished, some will emphasise, and see in this fact an explanation for some of Nyerere's apparent failings, especially in the sphere of democratic practice. After all, the world of African nationalism in the 1950s and 1960s, like so many other political worlds, was a hard world, filled, albeit not exclusively, with hard and ruthless men (and I also use the latter word advisedly). Nyerere, it could be argued, was a good man surrounded by many who did not quite share his vision or his high sense of moral purpose. And there is something in this. Certainly I recall, from reasonably close at hand, the struggle in the late 1960s over the succession to Mondlane with FRELIMO, the Mozambican liberation movement still primarily domiciled on Tanzanian soil. The outcome, that saw the far more worthy Samora Machel defeat the Simango faction, was won primarily because Nyerere had the political will and craft to back down the "cultural nationalist" triumvirate, so strong within TANU at the time, of Munanka, Sijaona and Maswanya, a group who sought, initially, to have the Tanzanian state guarantee Simango's ascendancy.

But this example also demonstrates the kind of power Nyerere could exercise when he cared to do so. The fact remains that if Nyerere is to be granted much of the credit for Tanzania's accomplishments he must also take his fair share of the blame for its more unsavoury by-products. But what blame? It has been argued (by Cran Pratt most eloquently perhaps and quite recently, in his essay with Hevina Dashwood in Bob Mathews and Taisier Ali's *Civil Wars in Africa*[3]) that Nyerere's political project was a judicious initiative that found, at least momentarily, in the so-called "democratic one-party state" a way of staving off the divisive tendencies — ethnic, regional, religious — that elsewhere have torn African polities apart. I even recall the theoretical acrobatics that Jonathan Barker and I performed in trying to make a related point about the judicious balance between the simultaneous imperatives of leadership and mass action that defined the 1970 Tanzanian election. I think in retrospect, as I shall suggest in a moment, we probably tried a little too hard to make that argument — although it also behooves me, before now making some more critical points about Nyerere's undemocratic practices than I was inclined to make in the late 1960s, to acknowledge the importance of the manner of his eventual departure from politics: his charms, like Prospero's, all o'erthrown, he retired gracefully to the sidelines, opening the way to his successor while also sanctioning the transition to an electoral process far more open, at least in formal terms, than the one he had himself fostered.

And yet there is something missing from an account so structured, if one allows for the moment the cold wind of reality to blow through it. I myself have very personal memories of the invasion of the campus at the University of Dar es Salaam by the field-force unit in 1970 and my student, the Kenyan leader of the University Student Council, Akivaga, being dragged at gunpoint down the steps of the central administrative building, then being tossed like a sack of old clothes in an army vehicle and sped away to expulsion both from the university and from the country. Nor can one forget firsthand accounts — but by then I wasn't there, having, with many others, not had our contracts renewed at the university — when protesting students were savagely beaten by security forces as they marched down the Morogoro road to town in 1978. Or take the case of my colleague Arnold Temu, the Tanzanian historian, first humiliated, even though an MP, for being one of a mere handful of Tanzanians who spoke out at the time of Akivaga's expulsion, and who, having rehabilitated himself sufficiently to become Dean of Arts at the time of the 1978 protest, was then summarily dismissed, sent into effective exile as an itinerant historian moving from Nigeria, to Swaziland, to the University of the Western Cape in South Africa. Is it a kind of paternalism, or perhaps a certain brand of residual Stalinism, that made it so difficult for many of us on the left to take full account of the import of such actions?

Or perhaps something else was behind this undemocratic tick, at least in the case of Nyerere himself. Years ago, I introduced a review of a volume of Nyerere's writings by citing Lenin's statement about George Bernard Shaw: "a good man fallen among Fabians." I meant to refer to the studied blandness of some of his least convincing statements about "socialism as an attitude of mind" and the like. But there may be another way of thinking this *bon mot* with reference to Nyerere, as I was reminded by an e-mail from a friend, himself once a Dar es Salaam academic, who reflected on what he chose to term "Nyerere's authoritarianism". How to explain it? He refers to the missionary influence and suggests, too, that "the notion of 'mwalimu' of the nation has always seemed to have a particularly missionary resonance: the shepherd and his flock, perhaps combining with certain aspects of patriarchal authority in indigenous culture (more commonly remarked). My feelings about this aspect of Nyerere also draw on observation of his style on certain occasions at UDSM when I was there: the way he handled 'critical' questions from the left, etc. — very much in the manner of the tolerant but potent teacher/leader, adjudicating what could be said and how." Interestingly, in looking back over some of my own early writings in preparation for this conference I found that I had made almost precisely the same point thirty years ago about the style of Nyerere in his visits to the Hill.

But what of the "fallen among Fabians" reference? "Are you familiar with the Cowen and Shenton thesis on 'Fabian colonialism?'" my e-mail correspondent asks. "It gives a new and interesting twist to colonial paternalism/benevolent authoritarianism — the need to deliver to Africans the benefits of bourgeois civilization while 'protecting' them from its costs (above all, divisive class formation), not least, of course, by 'adapting' African custom to the new circumstances and other modes of state intervention in and regulation of the conditions of social (and 'moral') existence. I suspect that these factors/forces of liberal colonialism/missionary endeavour have been overlooked in the formation of both Nyerere's ideas and practices."

I would suggest, then, that these ingredients and others helped produce an often unattractively undemocratic edge to Nyerere's politics. Nor can I ignore other evidence of Nyerere's fist beneath the velvet glove well beyond the Hill in Dar es Salaam. For example, in studying the evolution of the hard, authoritarian practices that characterised the politics of SWAPO in exile and that culminated in the nightmarish torture and killings in SWAPO's camps in Angola in the 1980s, it is difficult to lose sight of Nyerere's fingerprints all over the history that produced this outcome (in the Tanzanian state's incarceration of SWAPO cadres who dared to ask embarrassing questions of the SWAPO leadership at Kongwa in the mid-1960s, for example). Even more dramatic was the transfer from Zambia to Tanzania of the eleven most prominent spokespersons of the democratic movement that had sprung up in Zambia to, once again, question a corrupt and unresponsive SWAPO leadership. Rounded up by the Zambian army they were eventually spirited away, at SWAPO request, to Dar es Salaam where they could be unceremoniously left to rot in jail, precisely because Tanzania did not have the nuisance factor of Zambia's *habeus corpus* provisions. Here was Nyerere presiding, not very benignly, over what Colin Leys and I came to term the "Club of Presidents", a club that linked national leaders and liberation movement leaders around a common desire to block off, often in the most brutal possible way, the seeds of any dissent that led outside a very limited circumference of acceptable discussion.

I'm also struck, more anecdotally, by the story that I once heard the late, estimable Zanzibari/Tanzanian politician Mohamed Babu tell at a public forum during his years of effective exile from his home country, a story about his own arbitrary detention during the 1970s and his own languishing, without benefit of hearing or trial, in a Dodoma prison for a number of years. One night (on his account), as the radio played on loudspeakers through the darkened prison, a BBC interview with Nyerere was broadcast, an interview in which, answering a direct question, the President stated that there were no political prisoners in Tanzania. Instantly, through the darkness, the voice of a fellow detainee, ex-army officer Ali Mafoudh, rang through the prison to the delight of the others: "Nani sisi? Mbuzi?" Amusing at one level, of course, but it is also the kind of textural specificity to the reality of "one-party democracy" that is too often missing from our discussions.

Even more important, however, is the way in which this discussion can and must be brought back to further illuminate our evaluation of Nyerere's socialist project. Of course, the manner, outlined above, in which the students were dealt with was emblematic enough; they were after all, and on both occasions when force was used against them, asking that the leadership act more effectively to implement the democratic injunctions and anti-corruption rules that were ostensibly in place within the national polity. And the workers, without effective unions in the first place and then crushed — arrested, shipped off to the rural areas — at the Mount Carmel Rubber Factory in 1973, were also making, in the spirit of Mwongozo, the TANU Guidelines, much the same democratic demands. But Mount Carmel was, in any case, merely the most extreme example of the tight stranglehold that TANU held over the organisation of workers, women and the like on Nyerere's watch.

There is, finally, an even more emblematic moment with reference to which I will close my discussion: the shutting down of the Ruvuma Development Association (RDA) in 1969. This is not a moment that finds much resonance in most writing about Tanzania, although fortunately Andrew Coulson in his book on Tanzania does include an extended and extremely insightful appendix that gives the RDA and its demise its due weight.[4] I say that I find the moment emblematic, although, to be honest, I'm not quite certain whether it marked a turning point in and of itself or instead merely epitomised clearly the limits on the vision — Nyerere's? TANU's? — that underpinned the *ujamaa* project in the first place. In any case, the incident does warrant a great deal of thinking about.

In Ruvuma, after all, was to be found grass-roots empowerment of a very real and tangible kind — in the rural development sphere, in the education sphere, even in the sphere of local-level industrialization — a perfect example of the kind of "street-level democracy" (albeit the "streets" were a few dusty roads in one of the most economically backward parts of the country) whose importance Jonathan Barker has highlighted in his powerful recent book of that title.[5] The RDA also embodied a process that Nyerere himself, for a time, seemed to take strength from as he developed his overall socialist project, and, centrally, his specific vocation for rural socialism, in the late 1960s. Let me, to make a long and crucially important story short, merely quote the conclusion of Andrew Coulson's account:

> Given this support, the decision to disband the Association [RDA] could only be taken at the national level. In 1969 the Central committee of TANU was reformed, to include a majority of members elected by regional party branches. Thus professional politicians from the regions suddenly achieved power at the centre of the Party. In July 1969 the new Committee met in Handeni to discuss ujamaa for a whole month, and decided that its members would spend five weeks living in some of the most advanced villages in the country, including four of the RDA villages. These visits confirmed their worst fears: the RDA was an autonomous organization receiving funds and person-nel from abroad, and promoting a form of socialism which did not depend on a strong central party. If RDA organizations became the norm nationally, the professional politicians would be in a far weaker position. Moreover, by 1969 another model was available, much more attractive to them: good reports were coming in from the Rufiji valley, the first large-scale movement of all the people of an area into planned villages. This was organised by party officials (rather than by any grass-roots organization of the peasants) and gave the officials an obvious sense of achievement. It was soon to become the policy nationally, and it was entirely incompatible with the existence of groups of independent, politicized peasants, such as those of the RDA villages, which would be small, voluntary and might well oppose central direction. On 24 September 1969 the Central Committee met in Dar es Salaam, under Presi-dent Nyerere's chairmanship, and 21 out of its 24 members voted in favour of disbanding the RDA.

> There was little or no planning as to how this decision would be implemented. On 25 September the Minister for Rural Development and Regional Administration flew by government plane to Songea, with members of the Central Committee, to announce the decision to the people. The assets of the Association were confiscated — the grain mill, the sawmill, the mechanical workshop, vehicles and equipment. The police were sent to take away any Association property in the villages. The expatriate staff left quietly within a few days. The villagers got on with their work as best they could. Within a

week the teaching staff in the school was transferred to posts throughout the country— to Mara, Kigoma, Mbeya, Dodoma, and Singida regions. The model for Freedom and Development and Education for Self-Reliance had been destroyed.

I was reminded just last week by my friend from Tanzanian days, and then colleague for over twenty-five years at Atkinson College, Grif Cunningham, that just as the events described by Coulson were building up he (Grif) had been appointed, from his post as principal of Kivukoni College, to be special presidential advisor to the President on *ujamaa* villages. A firsthand student of Tanzanian rural development for many years, and not least of the whole Ruvuma experience, Grif was on a brief leave in Canada when the decision to close the RDA was taken. He arrived back in Tanzania to find that, with the decision to close down grass-roots democracy as an essential building block of rural transformation his job was, as he was told upon his return to Dar, now pretty much null and void. He spent the two years of his contract more or less in limbo as the disastrous policy of forced villagization gathered steam, tolling, as we can now see, the death knell of any democratic socialist aspiration in the country.

For me the lesson is clear, albeit, speaking personally, it has been a painful and difficult one for me to learn over the years, and I learned it perhaps even more as a fellow traveler of FRELIMO's post-liberation left-developmental socialist project than I did in Tanzania. A socialist aspiration of some kind — a challenge to the illogic of actually-existing capitalism, both globally and as it works its malign purposes on the African continent itself— must, it seems to me, be at the core of any meaningful response that Africa is eventually to make to the crisis in which it finds itself. We learn that positive lesson from, amongst others but not least, Julius Nyerere. But, as that aspiration reemerges politically, it must be a far more democratic project than anything Africa has witnessed in the name of socialism heretofore. In the end, and with all necessary qualifications, we learn that negative lesson, too, from, amongst others but not least, Julius Nyerere.

Endnotes

1 Dodd, William Atherton. *Education for Self-Reliance in Tanzania: A Study*. New York: Columbia University Teachers College Press, 1969.

2 Tanzania. *Socialism and Rural Development*. Dar es Salaam: Government Printer, 1967.

3 Ali, Taisier and Matthews, Robert O., eds. *Civil Wars in Africa: Roots and Resolution*. Montreal: McGill-Queen's University Press, 1999.

4 Coulson, Andrew, ed. *African Socialism in Practice: The Tanzanian Experience*. Nottingham: Spokesman, 1979.

5 Barker, Jonathan, Cwikowski, Anne-Marie, Gombay, Christie, Isbester, K., eds. *Street-Level Democracy: Political Settings at the Margins of Global Power*. Toronto and West Hartford, Conn.: Between the Lines and Kumarian Press, 1999.

CHAPTER THREE

The Challenge of Development in Tanzania:

THE LEGACY OF JULIUS NYERERE

Julius E. Nyang'oro

There are many ways to assess the legacy of President Julius Nyerere in Tanzania and beyond. At one extreme, we could blame him for all the economic ills that Tanzania has faced in the last quarter century and proclaim that he might have been the worst thing to happen to Tanzania. Certainly, there are people who feel that way.[1] At the other extreme, there are those who might be tempted to glorify everything Nyerere did, defending or overlooking the worst aspects of his regime and blaming other forces — internal or external — for the ills of Tanzanian society.

A more useful analysis of Nyerere's legacy, however, requires a recognition of the complexity of Julius Nyerere the person (his personal background, education and life experiences), the complexity of the development process and the challenges of leading a country that is underdeveloped, and the complexity of the international system that both Nyerere as leader, and Tanzania as a country, found themselves in after independence. I propose that every aspect of Tanzania's development, particularly between 1961, when Tanzania's mainland (Tanganyika) gained independence and 1985, the year Nyerere voluntarily retired from the presidency, must be viewed in this condensed complexity in order to come to grips with what his legacy would be in terms of the discourse of development and the practice of development in Africa.

Analytically, acknowledging this condensed complexity allows us the opportunity to appreciate the enormity of the task of 'development'. Such an approach also gives us the license to disaggregate the condensed complexity in ways which make sense to individual analysts who in turn are not held hostage to a particular "standard" in approaching the subject of Nyerere and his legacy. This is the approach I am adopting for this paper.

The paper is divided into two broad parts. The first deals with the critical aspects of development in Tanzania during Nyerere's regime. The second part is an analysis of politics in Tanzania during his rule.

The Tyranny of Political Economy

As president of a new country, Julius Nyerere inherited a political economy that can be described as an underdeveloped economy *par excellence*. The features of such a political economy have been made famous by the "underdeveloped" school. In the case of Africa, Walter Rodney's 1989 book *How Europe Underdeveloped Africa*[2] remains a classic treatise on how the historical linkage between the "centres" of global capitalism and the "periphery" has played itself out, resulting in the miserable economic condition in which Africa finds itself today. Predictably, Rodney took a long historical view of the linkage between early European expansion both to the Americas and to Africa with the massive exploitation of African labor in the form of the Atlantic slave trade and, later, colonial control of African labor on the continent. As Rodney put it:

> Colonial Africa fell within that part of the international capitalist economy from which surplus was drawn to feed the metropolitan sector. Exploitation of land and labour is essential for human social advance, but only on the assumption that the product is made available within the area where the exploitation takes place. Colonialism was not merely a system of exploita-

tion, but one whose essential purpose was to repatriate the profits to the so-called 'mother country'. From the African viewpoint, that amounted to consistent expatriation of surplus produced by African labor out of African resources. It meant the development of Europe as a part of the same dialectical process in which Africa was underdeveloped.[3]

The resulting characteristics of such a political economy were obviously a matter of concern for a leader who had a commitment to the general welfare of the population. The first characteristic that needed correction was an economy that was highly imbalanced between production and consumption. Indeed, the old adage that underdeveloped economies usually produce what they do not consume, and consume what they do not produce, accurately described Tanzania's economy at the time of independence. All the essential consumer goods such as soap, bicycles, clothing, etc., were either imported from Europe — particularly Britain — or from the more industrially developed neighbour, Kenya. Historically, Kenya had played the role of the "centre of the periphery" for East Africa within the general framework of the East African High Commission, and later, the East African Common Services Organization (EACSO). In later years, the structure of EASCO and its successor, the East African Community (EAC), became a bone of contention among the member countries (Kenya, Uganda and Tanzania), leading to the breakup of the community in 1977.

The breakup of the EAC can partly be explained by the unhappiness of Tanzania under Nyerere, of the disadvantages suffered by Tanzania in terms of the allocation of industries and services in the community which continued to reflect the imbalance between production and consumption. Before his death, Nyerere had again taken up the cause for the creation of a new and more equitable community, but that objective is yet to be achieved.

The second characteristic of the Tanzania political economy that needed attention was the overall development strategy. As has been noted by many scholars,[4] the colonial state had given little consideration to what really happened to producers of surplus in the colonial economies. In the case of Tanzania, the overwhelming majority of producers were peasants who lived in isolated villages across the country, and yet were coordinated by the colonial production machine. Peasant producers had been brought into the colonial nexus through the colonial state's imposition of taxes and cash crops and the general facilitation by the state of the colonial economy. At the time of independence little had been achieved in the sense of the general welfare of the population. There were, for example, only 12 fully qualified local doctors in the country (which meant a ratio of 1:870,000). The infant mortality rate was 225 per 100 births, life expectancy was 35 years and less than half the population was literate.

Naturally, Nyerere saw these development realities as something that needed immediate attention. His initial discussion of "*ujamaa*" as a voluntary communal development strategy was based on his belief that peasants in Tanzania would see the wisdom of communal production, especially if it was also tied to a state strategy of rationalising and centralising the delivery of essential services. To bring a global flavor to his development strategy for rural Tanzania, Nyerere visited a number of "socialist" countries, including the People's Republic of China, North Korea and Yugoslavia. By the end of 1966, however, it was clear to Nyerere that the voluntary aspects of villagization, and the supposed benefits to accrue to peasants had not really taken root in the psyche of Tanzanians in general. At the same time, it was becoming increasingly clear to Nyerere that the international community (i.e., the capitalist world) was not going to come through in terms of massive economic aid to Tanzania. As a result, through the ruling party's principal decision-making organ (the National Executive Committee), he adopted a sweeping development strategy under the general title of *The Arusha Declaration*. Perhaps the most striking statement of Arusha was that the "policy of TANU is to build a socialist state."[5] It could be argued that this single statement catapulted Tanzania into global controversy, and may have sealed the country's fate in relation to the capitalist world, even though Nyerere himself had viewed socialism only as an ideal that Tanzania should aspire to. In *The Arusha Declaration*, Nyerere stated that:

> A truly socialist state is one in which all people are workers and in which neither capitalism nor feudalism exists. It does not have two classes of people, a lower class composed of people who work for their living, and an upper class of people who live on the work of others. In a really socialist country, no person exploits another; everyone who is physically able to work does so; every worker obtains a just return for the labour he performs; and the incomes derived from different types of work are not grossly divergent.[6]

More than any other policy or statement, *The Arusha Declaration* was the beginning of a process that lasted until 1985 when Nyerere retired from the presidency. Internationally, the statement made him a lightning rod for the new wave of socialist-inspired rhetoric coming out of Africa. Indeed, Nyerere's statement had been a culmination of two processes: one internal, the other external. Internally, the president had been confronted with the reality of underdevelopment that defied easy solutions. Further, peasants who had been the target of voluntary *ujamaa* had not responded to villagization in large measure. The new elite at the University of Dar es Salaam had demonstrated against policies that sought to limit their privileges once they graduated, and Nyerere, in his capacity as chancellor of the university and president of the country, had expelled the majority of university students for demonstrating against his initiative to limit the benefits of the emerging *petite bourgeoisie* class.

Externally, Nyerere had been confronted by three major developments. First in 1965, Ian Smith, along with his white compatriots in Rhodesia, unilaterally declared independence (UDI) from Britain. Nyerere saw Smith's act as a rebellion that should be immediately quashed by Britain. When Britain refused to do so, Nyerere broke off diplomatic relations with Britain and, in the process, any foregoing British economic aid. Secondly, in 1964, the two countries of Tanganyika and Zanzibar formed a union resulting in the new country of Tanzania. Tanganyika, under Nyerere, had had diplomatic relations with West Germany. The Revolutionary Government of Zanzibar, meanwhile, had had diplomatic relations with East Germany. With the Union, West Germany demanded that Tanzania cut off diplomatic relations with East Germany. When Tanzania refused the request, West Germany cut off all aid to Tanzania. Thirdly, most of the money expected from the West for purposes of economic development simply did not come through. A combination of these factors led Nyerere to the idea of "self-reliance" as a basis for development.

It is possible, then, to see that while Nyerere has at times been accused of being a socialist radical most of the policy measures he undertook were clearly in response to events over which he had little control. It would be erroneous therefore, to view his ideology and policies as those of a radical socialist. Rather, it would be more accurate to describe him as an ambitious pragmatist who decided to do something about development. His lack of success in creating a dynamic economy and his difficulties in solving major development problems could thus be attributed more to the structural realities of Tanzania's political economy than to a lack of vision. Indeed, his frustrations were engendered by both the local and external environments.

Early in his presidency Nyerere realised the difficulties associated with structural constraints in implementing a development strategy that would attack underdevelopment. His international experience, derived from both travel and his student days in Great Britain, forced upon him the conclusion that the only way Tanzania could catch up with the developed world was for Tanzania to speed up its pace of development, while the rest of the world maintained a "normal pace". Thus was born the phrase "We must run while they walk."[7]

As we look back at the philosophy of "running while others walk", we can safely conclude that this was Nyerere's attempt to "cheat" the presumed normal operations of the political economy. "Running" in part, meant that Tanzanian society should try to squeeze surpluses out of an economy whose primary technological tool in development was the hoe. The two principal mechanisms for this transformation after 1967 became villagization, primarily as a mechanism for pooling of resources and better communal organization in production, and direct state intervention in the management of the economy, primarily in the urban sector. It took Nyerere six years after *The Arusha Declaration* to realise that voluntary movement by peasants to *ujamaa* villages would not happen quickly enough to allow him to "cheat" the system — and thus the forced villagization that took place between 1972 and 1973 with disastrous consequences for the economy.[8]

Political Economy and Development Strategy: Lessons Learned

While state centrality may not be a universally accepted strategy for economic development its importance as an instrument of societal governance cannot be overstated. The state in developed capitalist economies plays a pivotal, if not vital, role in ensuring governance. Thus in modern society state intervention, at least minimally, is to be expected, if not outright desirable and necessary. Arguably, under conditions of underdevelopment, the state becomes even more important as a vehicle for societal organisation and as an instrument for economic development. Yet, the role to be played by the state in economic organization has been one of the most difficult points of contention between the Bretton Woods institutions and many Third World countries, including Tanzania. This certainly was one of the biggest problems between Nyerere and the International Monetary Fund and the World Bank. It is fair to conclude that as it became increasingly clear to him that he was losing the ideological battle because of the overwhelming force of neoliberalism, Nyerere sought the most gracious way to exit, which was retirement.

Yet, it is also fair to note that state centrality for Nyerere was not for its own sake, but rather was a necessary aspect of a development strategy to speed up capital accumulation and surplus production. It was only through such a strategy, he argued, that more schools, hospitals, roads, etc., could be built. Thus, the massive government decentralization project enunciated in 1972 can be understood as part of this strategy. Decentralization was a program that physically transferred staff and many senior government officials from headquarters (Dar es Salaam) to the regions and administered centrally through the Prime Minister's Office. Along with villagization, decentralization was the other pillar for rapid rural development. But decentralization has been criticised as one way in which the state moved to take away local power. Andrew Coulson, for example, has argued that:

> The 'decentralization' of July 1992 could equally well have been called 'centralization'; for it meant the end of local government, which was replaced in each region and district by an arm of the central civil service, under the Prime Minister's Office....The word 'decentralization' refers not to power, but to staff: many senior officials were 'decentralized'.[9]

Predictably, decentralization met with little success, especially in the critical area of assisting in the villagization project. Decentralized bureaucrats for the most part still paid their allegiance to the centre (headquarters) and did little listening to the villagers who were intended as the beneficiaries of decentralization. The presumption of decentralization had been that more local input would be sought in any development activity. But, as was the case before, most resources were still concentrated at the centre.

Overall, the development strategy of Nyerere met with little success. The question is why was this the case? The answer could be derived from a further three questions which were posed by Lionel Cliffe and John Saul.[10] Simply stated, the two authors noted that with state centrality as the basis for economic development under global capitalism:

a) how could a policy of socialism and self-reliance be reconciled with continued aid from the West, and even from such bodies as the World Bank?;

b) as regards the nature of Tanzania's industrial strategy; did the emphasis on rural development create a permanent turning away from heavy industry? What were the costs and benefits of partnerships or management contracts with large foreign capitalist concerns?;

c) as regards the policy of *ujamaa vijijini* (villagization-socialism and rural development) what were to be the actual detailed format of the "frontal" transformation of the different rural areas in Tanzania to centers of cooperative production and what were to be the means for realizing that end?

As Cliffe and Saul noted, and indeed as Nyerere himself had recognised early on, the nature of the international system was going to be one of the major obstacles in achieving his development strategy. Prices of Tanzania's exports on the world market continued to fall, and there was the increasing unwillingness of international donors to support Tanzania's deficit spending. Furthermore, the uncertainties and economic insecurities on the part of Tanzanian peasants led many of them — through passive resistance such as non-production — to pursue production strategies which concentrated on food commodities as opposed to cash crops. Thus, the internal environment unwittingly conspired with external pressure to thwart many of Nyerere's goals.

Perhaps the best lesson Nyerere learned from the failures of his development strategy is a lesson that he had taken to heart as early as 1963. In a seminal essay in the inaugural issue of the *Journal of Modern African Studies*, Nyerere[11] noted the hopelessness of a development strategy that did not include African unity as its central tenet. In an ironic twist, one of the last major speeches he made before he fell ill in 1997 was to the South African Parliament in which he observed that as globalisation continues apace and as sub-Saharan Africa's participation in it is minimal (less than 5 percent of global trade), the only answer for Africa may come from pooling resources and developing a strategy that is continental.[12] In sum, if Tanzania is to develop under globalism, it has to be part of a broader African agenda. It is a lesson that clearly has not been appreciated by most of the current leadership on the continent.

Tanzanian Politics Under Nyerere: The Triumph of Corporatism?

I have argued that Tanzania under Nyerere presented an interesting paradox in the practice of politics in Africa, the paradox being that the Tanzanian state was among the few in Africa that for a long time managed to maintain a liberal image while at the same time establishing a virtual organisational hegemony over its working people and 'popular' classes. Even more perplexing were the relatively few instances of direct confrontations between the state and 'civil society'.

Part of the reason for the state's success can be traced to the strength of the Tanzanyika African National Union (TANU) at the time of independence and the skill with which President Nyerere managed to bring to his side the most prominent politicians in the country. Nyerere was able to incorporate into the government and ruling party structure both the Tanzania Federation of Labor (TFL) and the Cooperative Movement (CM). TFL and CM would have been the most effective challengers to state power had they been allowed to flourish outside the party structure. By adopting the strategy of incorporating potential challengers to state power Nyerere was adopting a corporatist strategy which had grave implications for how politics would be practiced in Tanzania, interest articulation of a very particular kind given what the practice of corporatism entails:

> Corporatism refers to a particular set of policies and institutional arrangements for structuring interest representation. Where such arrangements predominate, the state often charters or even creates interest groups, attempts to regulate their number, and gives them the appearance of a quasi-representational monopoly along with special prerogatives. In return for such prerogatives and monopolies the state claims the right to monitor representational groups by a variety of mechanisms so as to discourage the expression of "narrow" class-based, conflictual demands. Many state elites past and present have used such corporatist policies for structuring interest representation.[13]

It is possible to sell a corporatist strategy to civil society if material gains are readily identifiable, and Nyerere's early rhetoric on economic development and welfarism indeed served this purpose as the population at large identified the ruling party with material gains in the form of hospitals, schools and other welfare benefits. But as the economy started to perform poorly beginning in the early 1970s there was no longer a guarantee of popular support for corporatist politics. Nevertheless, there was a considerable lag between the beginnings of economic decline and popular unhappiness with the Nyerere regime. This lag could partly be explained as the success of the *ujamaa* ideology. *Ujamaa* was not only an economic development strategy, it was a rallying point for nationalism.

Some critics have agreed that Nyerere's Tanzania followed the classic pattern of authoritarian states in using ideology as a mechanism for gaining legitimacy. According to Clive Thomas,[14] there are four principal ways in which the state can use ideology to justify and cushion its authoritarian character. First, because of the highly fragmented and disarticulated production structures, combined with the non-resolution of the national question, the state promotes itself as the principal unifying force and unifying symbol of the society. Second, the relative recentness of political independence has led to the promotion of the state as a unifying symbol, thus reinforcing its claims to exercise sovereignty on behalf of the country in the international sphere. Third, the state is invariably promoted as an institution "above and beyond class", representing in effect a simple equation of state and society. Fourth, the emphasis on the goals of development and modernisation takes precedence over any consideration of social justice or democracy. The absence of social justice or democracy is explained as the necessary cost of development.

One may be tempted to conclude that Tanzania under Nyerere exhibited all four of the tendencies identified by Thomas, and thus Tanzania was an authoritarian state. Although I would consider this to be an overstatement, it is true that a combination of *ujamaa* ideology and corporatist arrangements under the ruling party were instruments of controlling political life by the state in Tanzania. One obvious consequence of the corporatist framework for Tanzania was the relatively slow pace of development of civil society. While ideologically one could argue that the Tanzanian population was active and aware of state policies, corporatist arrangements actually had the effect of organisationally demobilising civil society. Evidence of this organisational demobilisation is the difficulty that political opposition in Tanzania has faced in the multi-party era that began in 1992. By the middle of 2000, it was a foregone conclusion that the ruling party, Chama Chu Mapindazi (CCM), would handily win the October 29 general elections. Since the first multi-party elections in 1995, the opposition has suffered major losses, including the defection of opposition leaders back to CCM. In terms of multi-party politics, it is instructive to remember that it was Nyerere's party leader who publicly advised CCM to relinquish its monopoly of politics and allow for competition. It is reasonable to assume that he felt confident CCM would continue to win elections even under multi-partyism.

Conclusion

Nyerere's legacy in Tanzania is a mixed bag of vision, idealism and political commitment on the one hand, and failure to realise this vision on the other. Without question, his leadership was inspiring both nationally and globally, especially his commitment to peace and justice. Certainly his deeply religious background (he was Catholic) might have contributed to his sense of justice, but the reality of underdevelopment in Tanzania was critical in influencing his desire to become a radical reformer of the political economy. Given this condensed reality it would be a mistake to isolate a few cases of success or failure and judge him on that basis. While my essay does not touch upon his role as supporter of the liberation movement in Southern Africa, the liberation of Mozambique and Zimbabwe can certainly be placed on his resume as clear cases of success. Nonetheless, his contribution to the creation of a Tanzanian nation clearly marks him as the most important figure in Tanzanian politics in the twentieth century.

Endnotes

1 Hartmann, Jeannette. President Nyerere and the State, in *Tanzania After Nyerere*, ed. Michael Hood. London: Pinter, 1988.

2 Rodney, Walter. *How Europe Underdeveloped Africa*. Nairobi: Heinemann, 1989.

3 *Ibid.*, p.162.

4 Iliffe, John. *A Modern History of Tanganyika*. Cambridge: Cambridge University Press, 1979; Coulson, Andrew. *Tanzania: A Political Economy*. Oxford: Clarendon Press, 1982; Shivji, Issa. *Class Struggles in Tanzania*. New York: Monthly Review Press, 1976; Rodney, Walter. *How Europe Underdeveloped Africa*.

5 Nyerere, Julius K. *Freedom and Socialism/Uhuru na Ujamaa*. Dar es Salaam: Oxford University Press, 1968, p. 231.

6 *Ibid.*, p. 233.

7 Smith, William Edgett. *We Must Run While They Walk*. Harare: Zimbabwe Publishing House, 1981.

8 Hyden, Goran. *Beyond Ujamaa in Tanzania: Underdevelopment and an Uncaptured Peasantry*. Berkeley: University of California Press, 1980; Shao, John. "Politics and the Food Production Crisis in Tanzania." *Issue: A Journal of Opinion* 14: 10-24.

9 Coulson, Andrew. *Tanzania: A Political Economy*, p. 254.

10 Cliffe, Lionel and Saul, John, S., eds. *Socialism in Tanzania: An Interdisciplinary Reader Vol. 2: Policies*. Dar es Salaam: East African Publishing House, 1973, pp. 3-4.

11 Nyerere, Julius K. "A United States of Africa." *Journal of Modern African Studies* 1 (1): 1-6.

12 Nyerere, Julius K."Address to Members of Parliament: By Mwalimu Julius K. Nyerere, Cape Town, 16 October 1997." *Review of African Political Economy* 26 (82): 519-24.

13 Stepan, Alfred. *The State and Society: Peru in Comparative Perspective*. Princeton, NJ: Princeton University Press, 1978.

14 Thomas, Clive. *The Rise of the Authoritarian State in Peripheral Societies*. New York: Monthly Review Press, 1984.

CHAPTER FOUR

The Ethical Foundation of Julius Nyerere's Legacy

Cranford Pratt

Following the death of Julius Nyerere, there were, internationally, many expressions of the respect and affection that he had long commanded. Nevertheless, there intruded into these retrospective articles critical and sweeping judgments that, because of his socialist policies, Nyerere had not served his people well. At about the same time as I read these articles a moving letter from a close friend, who had long been an associate of Nyerere and who had returned to Tanzania to be present at Nyerere's funeral, led me to question these easy critical generalizations. She wrote:

> It was very sad but also awesome. The people went in their hundreds of thousands — more — wherever the coffin was. For the most part they stood in quietness. The grief was palpable. Honestly, millions of Tanzanians were involved because they wanted to be — to have some way of expressing their

feelings. The police just stood back and let them go where they wanted to, only gently keeping a path clear when necessary. Some people were crying but there was none of the formal wailing. For the most part it was the quietness, the standing in sorrow and slow movements afterwards which made me want to cry, at the same time as it stopped me from doing so. There was no pushing or shoving. I really cannot express their feeling or mine resulting. It was a depth of community mourning in which there was nothing formal or forced. It was individual as well as a coming together.

I was struck by the extraordinary contrast between the easy international criticisms and the profoundly different judgment of Tanzanians themselves to which this letter gives evidence. What were Tanzanians in their millions responding to, which the international commentators were ignoring?

The short answer is that Tanzanians have no doubt that for over forty years they had in their midst a leader of unquestionable integrity, who, whatever his policy errors, was profoundly committed to their welfare. That is the short answer and it is a good one. The long answer focuses on Nyerere's commitment to the welfare of his people. This commitment had generated the socialist initiatives which have been the primary focus of the criticisms of Nyerere's leadership leveled by western economists, governments and development agencies. Yet these initiatives emanated from that very commitment of Nyerere to his people's welfare which they so movingly acknowledged in their final farewell to him. It is in the different readings of the significance of that commitment that we can discover the reason for the contrast between the dominant western judgment of Nyerere and the judgment of his people.

I am not suggesting that Tanzanian socialism was in fact a great success and that this is recognised by the vast majority of Tanzanians, though not by most western observers. That would be both naive and inaccurate. Rather I am suggesting that while many of Nyerere's policy initiatives failed, they rested on an ethical foundation and on an understanding of the challenges which Tanzania faced, which were vastly more insightful than anything offered by his critics. An increasing number of students of African development are belatedly coming to recognise this truth. Perhaps, in contrast to them ordinary Tanzanians have always recognised it.

It will be argued here that a profound belief in the intrinsic equality of all humans was central to Nyerere's political values and that two of his most important legacies to his fellow Tanzanians flow from this belief in human equality — his emphasis on the democratic engagement of all citizens in the political life of Tanzania and his preoccupation with finding a development strategy for Tanzania which would neither generate severe income differences nor entrench class differences.

The Commitment to Equality

As just suggested, at the heart of Nyerere's political values was an affirmation of the fundamental equality of all humankind and a commitment to build social, economic and political institutions which would reflect and ensure this equality. This central emphasis on equality, we would hypothesise, had a variety of roots. It was in part shaped by his wide and eclectic reading while studying at the University of Edinburgh and in the years immediately after, readings in which classical liberalism, British socialism and Pan-African anti-colonialism were more prominent than Marxism.[2] More influential still were his reflections on the condition of his people. His aversion to both colonialism and racism, from his earliest adult years, both fuelled and was centrally founded upon a belief in human dignity and equality. For example, in the late 1950s when arguing the case for Tanganyikan[3] independence, he declared:

> Our struggle has been, still is, and always will be a struggle for human rights. As a matter of principle we are opposed and I hope we shall always be opposed to one country ordering the affairs of another county....Our position is based on the belief in the equality of human beings, in their rights and their duties as citizens.[4]

He swiftly had occasion to demonstrate that these sentiments were not mere rhetoric. In October 1960, only months before Tanganyika became independent, he battled successfully against strong sentiments in the Tanganyikan African National Union (TANU), that citizenship in an independent Tanganyika should be available only for Tanganyikan Africans but not for Tanganyikan Asians or Europeans. In an extemporaneous intervention in the National Assembly he declared:

> Discrimination against people because of their colour is exactly what we have been fighting against. This is what we formed TANU for, and so soon, sir...some of my friends...are preaching discrimination as a religion to us. And they

stand like Hitlers and begin to glorify the race. We glorify human beings, sir, not colour.[5]

Equally significant as a determinant of Nyerere's commitment to equality was the importance that he attached to the heritage of Tanzanians from their tribal past. Nyerere frequently presented his views on socialism as an expression of values which he felt to be an essential ethical component of African traditional societies.[6] The equality which Nyerere valued was not an equality of opportunity for essentially autonomous individuals but was rather the equality enjoyed in closely integrated and caring societies. This emphasis separated him from western liberalism, with its primary emphasis on individual liberty and its much weaker attention to equality and fraternity.

Nyerere recognised that the social values of traditional Tanzania were rapidly being undermined. He knew very well that the material ambitions of the emerging African bourgeoisie were powerful and hard to contain. He also knew that Tanzania would be poor for a very long time and that the building of a just society would become vastly more difficult if severe class differences were to become entrenched. From early on, Nyerere therefore argued that Tanzanians must find a way to progress economically that would not undermine the communal and egalitarian values which were central to their traditional heritage. They must build institutions within the wider society of their nation, which would preserve "the same socialist attitude of mind which in the tribal days gave to every individual the security that comes of belonging to a widely extended family."[7]

But would the new African elite be interested in building such a society? While income differences were still not vast within the African population of Tanzania, if primarily because Tanzania was still very poor, oligarchic ambitions and the morally corrosive power of consumer acquisitiveness had already begun to erode more socially responsible traditional values. From the earliest days of his leadership, Nyerere realised that his society needed modern educated men and women but that the members of this elite were bound to be tempted to set their aspirations by reference to the levels of material welfare enjoyed by the elites of other and much richer societies. One of his most insistent and recurrent themes was that the members of the new African elite had to remain intimately integrated within Tanzanian society and willing to advance in material well-being *together with*, rather than *vastly ahead* of ordinary Tanzanians.[8]

As early as June 1959, he declared:

> We are not going to enter the government to make money. We are condemned to serve, to wage war against poverty, disease and ignorance. I warn our future civil servants that they must think in terms of our country and not compare themselves with anyone outside his country....We shall slash the salaries of local people; if necessary we shall slash them hard.[9]

Two years later, when he realized that he would not receive the support of TANU colleagues for a radical assault upon the salary levels in the middle and upper levels of the public service, he exclaimed in exasperation, "[I]f there was a person on the moon he would say 'this government, they must be in serious love with their civil service.' "[10]

By the early 1960s Nyerere was convinced that Tanzania had, but only briefly, a unique opportunity to develop national political institutions and a national public ethic that would contain the selfish acquisitiveness of the bureaucratic and political elites. Without that he foresaw that Tanzania would quickly be "swamped by the temptation of personal gain or by the abuse of power by those by those in positions of authority."[11]

The Democratic One-Party State and its Legacy

In the first five years of independence Nyerere took several major initiatives that were a direct product of this concern to contain the economic and oligarchic ambitions of the political and bureaucratic elites. "The only way", he declared, "in which leadership can be maintained as a people's leadership is if the leaders have reason to fear the judgment of the people."[12]

Yet it was clear at that time that the ruling elite had little reason to fear either of the two institutions that in theory might have acted as effective watchdogs upon it: the party or parliament. With independence, the interest and personal ambitions of the party activists focused almost exclusively on the government and the National Assembly, because positions within them offered salaries that were substantial in Tanganyikan terms. TANU, the movement around which the great mass of Tanganyikans had mobilised and which they felt deeply a part of, seemed increasingly orphaned and without any clear role. Nyerere acted swiftly to try to correct this. On January 23,[rd] 1962, just 45 days after independence, he resigned as prime minister and for the next 11 months devoted himself entirely, as president of TANU, to a revitalisation of the party. He thus sought to counterbalance the unavoidable power of the new elite by a more effective moblisation of popular political power through the party, in a unifying national endeavour to build a new Tanganyika.[13]

Two years later he was ready to tackle the complex question of whether the Westminister-type parliamentary system, introduced by the British just as they were departing, was likely to produce a parliament which would be an effective instrument of popular control on the cabinet and government. Nyerere clearly thought not. Indeed he had swiftly recognised after independence how shallow and unsubstantial were the formal institutions of parliamentary democracy in Tanganyika. Not only was the Westminister model of constitutional government without roots but more specifically the single member constituency elections which took place under the 1960 constitution proved anomalous in the extreme. Because of the near universal popularity of TANU, its candidates were elected unopposed in 58 of the 78 constituencies in the 1960 election. As a result, a substantial majority of Tanzanians had no involvement at all in that election. More important still, party loyalty and the caution of MNAs, concerned about their political advancement, meant that although the president and cabinet were formally answerable to Parliament, it was rarely a significant constraint upon their exercise of power.

By 1965, TANU, under Nyerere's leadership, was ready to reorder the constitution of Tanzania, replacing the Westminister model with an original, hybrid constitutional order, the democratic one-party state.[14] It was a highly original effort to provide meaningful popular elections, greater answerability of the political leadership and genuine political participation by ordinary Tanzanians, while protecting Tanzania from the divisive ethnic, regional and religious factionalism which could easily destroy its fragile unity and which a fully open competition between rival parties might generate.

Its most original features establish that it was neither a subterfuge for oligarchic rule, the option preferred by many of the party elite, nor for an ideological vanguard party on the Leninist model. Membership in TANU was open to all, and any member could be nominated to run for the National Assembly or the representative organs of the party. In each constituency a large and representative body, the annual district conference of TANU, ranked the candidates for election to the National Assembly in order of preference. The National Executive Committee of the party then decided which two candidates would appear on the ballot, an arrangement which had the potential to become an instrument of oligarchic control but whose actual use, Nyerere ensured, was infrequent and unthreatening.[15] The elections which then followed operated within a set of rules that were designed to ensure as fair a contest as possible. No candidate could spend any money on his own campaign. All election meetings in every constituency were organised by the party and were to be addressed by both candidates. No tribal language could be used at these meetings and no appeal for votes could be made on grounds of race, tribe or religion. No politician or other prominent Tanzanian could campaign on behalf of any candidate.

Elections under this constitution clearly would not likely produce vigorous national debate on major national issues. Indeed the electoral system was designed to avoid the emergence of national factions, be they ideological, regional or tribal, and every effort had been made to keep the elections focused on the qualities of the local candidates. Nevertheless it did ensure that elected members of the National Assembly (MNAs), including cabinet ministers, would be answerable to the electorate at the next election. For example, in the first election under this constitution, 27 sitting members chose not to run, 13 members including 3 junior ministers failed to rank first or second in the district conference vote and therefore did not appear on the ballot, and a further 17 members of the previous parliament, including 2 ministers and 6 junior ministers, were defeated on election day. Thus 87 of the 103 elected members of the 1965 National Assembly had not been members of the previous parliament. Nyerere and his government had thus found a way for popular discontent to replace MNAs who had become unpopular, while avoiding the highly divisive impact which competitive party elections can have in countries whose national unity is fragile.

Although there was little or no support in Tanzania at that time for a return to a competitive democratic party system, a variety of factors came together to generate support for transforming Tanzania's democratic one-party democracy into a classic Leninist vanguard party. The case for a vanguard party, though primarily developed by non-Tanzanians at the University of Dar es Salaam,[16] did have some effective Tanzanian champions including a few within TANU. Some in the senior ranks of TANU were not averse to the legitimacy which an endorsation of TANU as a Leninist vanguard party would give to their own retention of power. The Maoist model, and in particular the austerity of the ruling Chinese elite and the markedly egalitarian character of Chinese society, attracted Nyerere's favorable attention. Many in TANU including Nyerere became impatient by the mid-1970s as it proved much more difficult than anticipated to persuade the rural population voluntarily to move from their scattered holdings into brand new villages and seriously to implement collective farming, the two initiatives which for several years absorbed a great deal of TANU's energy and, indeed, exhausted much of its political capital.

While the temptation to convert TANU into a vanguard party united by a firm ideological commitment to the early accomplishment of socialism was fed by factors such as those just listed, it is crucial to an understanding of Nyerere's legacy to Tanzania that it be recognised that he was always steadfastly opposed to TANU becoming a closed party of committed socialists, admitting to its membership only those whom it feels are fully committed to its doctrines. He argued down those who would rely on rule by an ideological elite to accomplish a socialist transformation. His belief in human equality, his recognition of the ease with which elites that are not answerable to the people become both corrupt and authoritarian and the value he attached to the participation of ordinary citizens in the nation's political processes finally ensured that the genuine democratic elements in the Tanzanian one-party democracy were retained and rule by a self-appointed ideological vanguard was avoided. Nyerere thus helped enormously to entrench within the Tanzanian political culture a belief that a wide range of political freedom must be retained and that political and social change must be sought through non-violent and constitutional political action.

The democratic one-party state was never without its flaws and contradictions. Recurrently there were detentions and human rights abuses that should never have been tolerated but were painfully defended by Nyerere as necessary for the stability of the nation.[17] Gradually the party became a party of the politically ambitious and less genuinely a "people's party" whose debates would convey to the leadership the sentiments of ordinary Tanzanians. Nevertheless, the 1965 constitution, reinforced by Nyerere's resistance to the lure of an ideological vanguard party, must be judged a major and positive legacy. For over 20 years it provided a largely unchallenged framework within which Tanzanians ordered their public affairs, enjoyed continuous and stable civilian rule and engaged in the public discussion of party and government policies more freely than was permitted in most African states at that time. Then, in the mid-1980s, peacefully and within the framework of this constitution, Nyerere stepped down, there was a change of political leadership and a transition to a competitive party system. These crucial changes were a realistic response to emerging Tanzanian aspirations, but their peaceful accomplishment owed much to the fact that they were strongly advocated by Nyerere. Since then, again through established political processes, though without Nyerere's active support, there has been nearly a 180-degree change in the direction of economic policies.

The Socialist Initiatives of 1967-76 and their Legacy

The political and constitutional reforms that produced and sustained the 1965 Constitution, however important, did little to address Nyerere's fundamental anxiety that Tanzania was failing to find a way to give modern and national expression to the equality and the social cohesion of traditional Tanzania. Indeed, with independence these anxieties intensified. In 1963, he wrote:

> We are committed to the philosophy of African socialism and basic to this is the principle of human equality. One of our concerns must therefore be to prevent the growth of a class structure in our society....We have developed an income structure in our society which is inconsistent with our declared aim of social equality....[W]e must prevent the present position from solidifying.[18]

These concerns moreover were widened to include political colleagues in addition to civil servants, for party officials demanded and received salaries and attractive perquisites of office that paralleled those of the public service. Party and government officials also began to seek ways to augment their income. As corruption goes, these were still small-scale — building second houses to be rented to foreign embassies and corporations, for example, and setting up on the side commercial farms to supply the urban markets. Nevertheless, undeniably, Tanzania was moving towards an increasingly stratified class system in which the dominant class would be the very political and bureaucratic elites which were to have ensured Tanzania a quite different future.

Nyerere also questioned the pattern of development that was proceeding in the rural areas. He feared that the cultivation of cash crops on single farm holdings would encourage individual acquisitiveness that it could not satisfy, would undermine communal values and would lead to rural class stratification and the creation of a rural, landless proletariat. Nyerere was therefore determined to "build up the countryside in such a way that our people have a better standard of living while living together on terms of equality and fraternity."[19]

The major socialist initiatives taken in 1967 and shortly thereafter reflected Nyerere's conviction that, unless these trends were swiftly reversed, Tanzania would soon have sacrificed any chance of creating modern national equivalents to its traditional communal and egalitarian values. He said of these socialist initiatives that, "had we delayed, you would discover two years from now that our leadership had become rather entrenched in the accumulation of personal property."[20]

Certainly the socialist measures were breathtaking in range and scope.[21] Moreover, they were accompanied by a major mobilisation of popular support to ensure that the new bourgeoisie would have little choice but to endorse them as well. Nyerere was seeking to place Tanzania irrevocably on the road to a genuinely socialist society. The banks, the foreign-owned plantations and important parts of the limited industrial sector were nationalised; an attempt was made to regulate a wide range of private economic activities; a stringent leadership code was introduced to contain corruption and to block the emergence of private economic activities by senior party and government leaders and officials; there was an extensive expropriation of household properties that were not occupied by their owners; a reform of the educational system was launched, designed to ensure that young Tanzanians would embrace the values and acquire the skills appropriate to a national society of equals; TANU took on the task of inducing peasants to farm collectively; and very large numbers of peasants were moved from their rural holdings to newly created villages.

Few now claim that many of these socialist initiatives were appropriate instruments for the development of a very poor country, especially not all at once and in a country whose public service was already over-extended. The leadership code irritated the political and governmental elite and was bypassed in a myriad of ways. Peasant farmers were resistant to communal farming on other than a token basis. The movement of rural peoples from their scattered holdings into villages alienated a great many. Many of the nationalised industries could only be run by engaging international corporations to manage them under contracts that had to be hurriedly negotiated by Tanzanians with little experience in international bargaining. The detailed regulation of a multitude of commercial and financial transactions proved beyond the competence of the civil service. Indeed, by the late 1970s Nyerere and TANU were themselves coming to recognise that many of these initiatives had proven inappropriate, indeed counter-productive, to the accomplishment of their objectives.

The critical view of Nyerere's socialist policies taken by the international financial institutions, by western governments and by most North American development economists has gone beyond criticisms of specific initiatives, to an impatient rejection of the very idea that Third World governments should seek actively to intervene in their economies either to advance social justice or to control the direction of their economic development. They have offered the Tanzanian experience as evidence, by counter-example, that African states must adopt a development strategy based on a minimal state, a market economy and full integration into the international capitalist economy.

Others today will, I am sure, address the intellectual crudity and ideological nature of this neoliberal view of the international economic policies that would best serve Tanzania's interests. What is offered here is the parallel argument that western judgments of Nyerere's domestic legacy have reflected political values which, in contrast to his, attach little importance to communities, are largely unconcerned with equality and are overwhelmingly preoccupied with economic growth. This perspective is also crude and has had consequences as disastrous for very poor countries as has the dominance of neoliberal international economic policies.

As a result, those concerned with the welfare of the peoples of the poorest countries are increasingly identifying as centrally important the generation of democratic controls and a robust public ethic that really do work, and the pursuit of development strategies that will equitably share throughout the whole society the material benefits they bring. These tasks, certainly, are not as straightforward as Nyerere had initially hoped. But we need to remind ourselves that it was not the World Bank, the IMF, the aid agencies of the industrialised states or mainstream western economists who had, decades ago, identified these central development challenges to the world's poorest countries. It was Julius Nyerere.

Endnotes

1 This chapter is a revised and expanded version of a similarly entitled article in the *Canadian Journal of African Studies*, vol. 33, no. 1, 1999.

2 Nyerere's Christian faith, while clearly important to him spiritually throughout his life, does not appear to have generated any detailed interest in Christian social and political thought, or at least not one to which he refers in his many writings of a more reflective and philosophical kind.

3 Tanzania has had several official names since it became independent in 1961. It was Tanganyika until 26 April 1964, the United Republic of Tanganyika and Zanzibar until the adoption of the 1965 Constitution and Tanzania since then.

4 From Nyerere's address in the Legislative Council on 16 December 1959. The text of this address is in Julius Nyerere, *Freedom and Unity: A Selection from Writings and Speeches*. Dar es Salaam and London: Oxford University Press, 1962, p. 75-80.

5 Tanganyika, *National Assembly Official Report*. 36th Session, vol. 1, cols 344-5, 18 October 1960.

6 The key text illustrating this is his 1962 booklet *Ujaama: The Basis of African Socialism*. Dar es Salaam, 1962. It is reprinted in his *Freedom and Unity*.

7 *Ujaama*, p. 7.

8 Two quotations may help to convey this component of his socialist convictions. In 1962 he wrote, "There are certain skills, certain qualifications, which for good reason command a higher rate of salary for their possessors than others....The true socialist will demand only that return for his skilled work which he knows is a fair one to the wealth or poverty of the whole society to which he belongs. He will not attempt to blackmail the community by demanding a salary equal to that paid to his counterpart in some far wealthier society" (*Ujamaa*, reprinted in *Freedom and Unity*, p. 169). A few years later he wrote, "[T]he first priority of production must be the manufacture and distribution of such goods as will allow every member of the society to have sufficient food, clothing and shelter, to sustain a decent life. ... Apart from these basic needs of man, a socialist society would put much emphasis on the production of socially advantageous goods. It would concentrate on better educational facilities, medical care, places of community activity like libraries, community centres and parks. It would devote resources also to social values that have nothing to do with production like improving the hours and conditions of work or maintaining the natural beauties of the world in which we live." (Introduction to *Freedom and Unity*, p. 11).

9 As quoted in Pratt, Cranford. *The Critical Phase in Tanzania, 1945-68: Nyerere and the Emergence of a Socialist Strategy*. Cambridge: Cambridge University Press, 1976, p. 218.

10 Tanganyika, *National Assembly Official Report* 36th Session, vol.5, col. 101, 10 October 1961.

11 *Ujamaa*, p. 12.

12 Introduction to *Freedom and Socialism*, p. 26.

13 In his first public explanation of his resignation, Nyerere declared that his goal was "the creation of a country in which the people take a full and active part in the fight against poverty, ignorance and disease" (*Tanganyika Standard* 23 January 1962 and quoted in Pratt, *The Critical Phase in Tanzania*, p. 116-17.

14 There was extensive interest in Tanzania's one-party democracy, much of it sympathetic. See for example Lionel Cliffe (ed.) *One Party Democracy.* Nairobi, East African Publishing House, 1967; Elections Study Committee, *Socialism and Participation: Tanzania's 1970 Election.s* (Dar es SalaamP: Tanzania Publishing House, 1974); John Saul, "The Nature of Tanzania's Political System: Issues Raised by the 1965 and 1970 Elections", Parts 1 and 2 in the *Journal of Commonwealth Political Studies* V, 2 and 3. It is also discussed at length in my *The Critical Phase in Tanzania, 1945-68: Nyerere and the Emergence of a Socialist Strategy.* (Cambridge: Cambridge University Press, 1976) and in Bismarck Mwansasu and Cranford Pratt (eds.). *Towards Socialism in Tanzania.* (Toronto: University of Toronto Press, and Dar es Salaam, Tanzania Publishing House, 1979).

15 Nyerere had acted swiftly to establish the practice that the NEC would normally accept that the top two candidates would appear on the ballot, thus ensuring that this power was not used to drop from the ballot candidates whose political views were disliked by the NEC. Instead it was used comparatively rarely and rather quaintly to exclude candidates whose addiction to alcohol or to corrupt practices was putatively widely known. This, I recall, was not totally reassuring to foreign observers such as myself but was at least not ideologically driven.

16 The most prominent of these included Andrew Coulson, Lionel Cliffe, Phillip Raikes, John Saul and Michaela von Freyhold.

17 Nyerere used an occasion which was bound to attract the interest of the international press and the diplomatic corps, the opening of the University College Dar es Salaam in August 1964, to offer an explanation along these lines of why he felt obliged on occasion to sign preventive detention orders. The text is presented in full in his *Freedom and Unity*, pp. 305-15.

18 From a speech of Nyerere's in February 1963, reprinted in *Vigilance Africa* 1(3), 1964 and quoted in Pratt, *The Critical Phase*, p. 226.

19 Nyerere, Julius. "Socialism and Rural Development", reprinted in his *Freedom and Socialism*, p. 346.

20 From a transcript of a press conference on 4 March 1967, quoted in Pratt, *The Critical Phase*, p. 236.

21 There is a remarkably extensive literature on Tanzania's socialist initiatives. The following book titles are presented in chronological order. Cliffe, Lionel and Saul, John, eds. *Socialism in Tanzania: An Interdisciplinary Reader.* Vols. 1 and 2. Nairobi: East African Publishing House, 1972 and 1973; Pratt, Cranford. *The Critical Phase in Tanzania*; Boesen, Jannik, Madsen, Bridgit and Moody, Tony. *Ujamaa: Socialism From Above.* Uppsala: Scandinavian Institute of African Studies, 1977; Mwansasu, Bismark and Pratt, Cranford, eds. *Towards Socialism in Tanzania.* Toronto and Dar es Salaam: University of Toronto Press and Dar es Salaam Publishing House, 1979; McHenry, Dean. *Tanzania's Ujamaa Villages: The Implementation of a Rural Development Strategy.* Berkeley: Berkeley Institute of International Studies, 1979; Coulson, Andrew. *African Socialism: The Tanzanian Experience.* Nottingham: Spokesman, 1979; Coulson, Andrew. *Tanzania: A Political Economy.* Oxford: Clarendon Press, 1982; Boesen, Jannik et al., eds. *Crisis and Struggle for Survival.* Uppsala: Scandinavian Institute of African Studies, 1986. There is also a vast literature of articles and chapters in books, including most recently Chapter 7 of James C. Scott's *Seeing Like a State: How Certain Schemes to Improve the Human Condition Have Failed.* New Haven: Yale University Press, 1998.

CHAPTER FIVE

An Economist's Reflections on the Legacies of Julius Nyerere

Gerry Helleiner

I spent some of the best years of my life working in Dar es Salaam in the late 1960s when Mwalimu Julius Nyerere was its inspiring young president. In later years, I worked for shorter periods in Tanzania — under each of its presidents — and had many occasions to reflect on the longer-term role that Nyerere played in his own country. Internationally, too, I have frequently had the honour and privilege of working in Mwalimu's ambit, most notably through the South Commission and the South Centre.

I believe I may be the only economist to speak at this conference. (In fact, it is quite possible that I am the only economist in attendance.) Much of the economics profession has taken rather a dim view of the legacy of Julius Nyerere. (I won't dignify with quotation or repetition some of the things I have heard said about him in the World Bank.) It is precisely *because* I am an economist — and

Mwalimu so evidently was not — that I want to put my profound admiration of his record and his legacy on the record.

It is undoubtedly in the field of economics that Julius Nyerere has received his worst press, and in which his legacy has been seen as most negative. The heading for his obituary in the (London) *Financial Times* read: "Man of integrity whose policies hurt his country." The obituary in *The Economist*, while generally friendly, concluded: "He was a magnificent teacher: articulate, questioning, stimulating, caring. He should never have been given charge of an economy." Personally, I see his legacy in the realm of economic and development policy rather differently.

Mwalimu's grasp of the traditional tenets of economic theory was probably weak and so was that of his closest advisors and speechwriters (although there were those within government of whom this could certainly not be said). Most of the criticism coming from economists relates to his 'socialist' policies. But his government's most damaging economic policy errors, in my view, had little to do with socialism *per se*. They came relatively late in his presidency and were on the relatively non-ideological issue of exchange rate policy; they were errors shared by many other low-income countries in the early 1980s.

As for his socialism, some elements can be faulted as far more serious in their negative economic consequences than others. Nationalisations and restrictions on competition (including price controls) in the trading, industrial, agricultural and financial sectors were far beyond governmental management capacities and proved costly. Widespread (and even forced) "villagization" in the rural sector was not only economically costly but also deeply unpopular. The "basic industry" policy — to the extent that it was part of Nyerere's 'socialism' — was also mistaken in that it was premature and inappropriate for so economically small a country; it too proved costly. All of these 'socialist' policies could be foreseen (and were) as likely to slow overall economic growth and development both immediately and over the longer run.[1] Arguably, none seemed likely, of themselves, however, to create the degree of economic collapse that occurred in the early 1980s. Nor, in my view, did they. Severe macroeconomic shocks — oil prices, weather, and war against Idi Amin in Uganda — and their serious domestic mismanagement were required for that.

In the early 1980s, as the UK White Paper on international development put it in its commentary on African experience, the "worldwide international climate...left little margin for policy errors."[2] In Tanzania, there undoubtedly were such policy errors. Again, my view is that Tanzania's economic dislocations in the early 1980s were only partially attributable to its efforts to restructure the economy towards socialism. Far more serious were the errors in macroeconomic policy in the face of severe shocks (as well as, of course, the shocks themselves).

It is important for critical economists (and others) to recall that there were other elements in Nyerere's socialist programme — increased equity in the distribution of income; an attempt at a direct assault on bottom-end poverty (including provision of primary education and clean water); a "leadership code" for politicians and civil servants; major reform of the educational syllabus; and (at least rhetorical) emphasis on self-reliance and reduced aid dependence. These elements of Nyerere's 'socialist' programme excited widespread admiration and support (ultimately too much support of an unhelpful kind) from many academics and policymakers in the capitalist West, particularly in the Nordic countries and the presidency of the World Bank. So compelling was this side of his socialist aspirations and practice that, for some time, admirers were prepared to give Tanzania the benefit of the doubt on the less propitious elements of its 'socialist' development policy and its economic sustainability. Sadly, as Tanzania's resource constraints tightened and macroeconomic policies faltered in the late 1970s and early 1980s most of these supporters lost confidence in the overall Nyerere socialist vision. Their withdrawal of financial support then worsened what had already become a crisis situation.

The first serious external pressures upon the government of Tanzania to reform its economic policies were related primarily to its macroeconomic management policies, *not* to its socialism, and they came, of course, from the IMF. According to the IMF tenets of the times, what Tanzania most required in the late 1970s and early 1980s was across-the-board governmental austerity and severe currency devaluation. It was the effort at imposition of such IMF conditionality that prompted Nyerere's famous public outburst (in 1981): "Who elected the IMF to be the Finance Ministry for every country in the world?" (or words to that effect). There followed an almost total breakdown in Tanzania-IMF relations. Julius Nyerere may be said to have fired the first African salvo in the great debate over the role of the IMF in Africa.

By a quirk of chance, it was at about the same time, 1980, that the annual meetings of the IMF were to be chaired by Amir Jamal, Tanzania's then-Minister of Finance. I remember his recounting his surprise when, upon his arrival in Washington for the meetings, IMF staff presented him with a draft of his introductory remarks. He thanked them for their thoughtfulness, he delighted in recalling, but told them he had brought his own speech.

At this point (1980-81), Nyerere and Tanzania were still sufficiently respected that the then-President of the World Bank, Robert McNamara, initiated a mediation effort to seek an accommodation between the IMF and the Tanzanians. This was to be attempted through the provision of technical assistance for the preparation, in Tanzania, of an alternative to the IMF's stabilisation and structural adjustment plan; the Government of Tanzania was given a voice (and indeed veto power) over the composition of the three-person team which was given the ultimate responsibility for the task. With both expatriate and local staff working together in Dar es Salaam for a year, an alternative structural adjustment programme was tortuously constructed. Anticipating later African debates, it called for much greater emphasis upon supply-side expansion than demand-side restraint; much greater care over the distributional effects of required macroeconomic adjustment (with conscious effort to maintain equity of sacrifice); and a more gradual programme for the implementation of reforms. The effort failed, however, when neither the government of Tanzania nor the IMF found the programme satisfactory. (Upon personally welcoming the agreed three-person team to Tanzania as it embarked on its task, the president followed his initial niceties to the group, each of whom he knew, with the prescient introductory substantive comment: "You know, gentlemen, I asked for money, not advice!" A more succinct statement of the problem of conditionality has probably never been made.)

A major sticking point in the failure to agree on what was, for its time, a highly innovative programme (as well as a potentially important model for IMF-member country dispute resolution), though not the only one, was the government's (mistaken) reluctance sufficiently to devalue its currency. I am personally convinced that, like so many laymen, Mwalimu did not understand the role of the exchange rate; some (not all) of his advisors gave him very bad advice.

As the government went ahead on its own, more and more donors (including now the World Bank) lost faith in Tanzanian macroeconomic management, the economy spiralled further downward, corruption grew, and all-around confidence in the entire Nyerere vision was lost. The advent of Reagan-Thatcher influences on economic policy throughout the world and in the Bretton Woods institutions (McNamara left the World Bank in 1981) furthered darkened external views of the Tanzanian situation.

The necessary policy turnaround — now in much more dire economic circumstances, and with both much more external policy leverage and, significantly, a degree of non-governmental (mainly university) technical influence — finally began in 1986, *after* Nyerere's departure. When the turnaround came, except for exchange rate action, which, by its nature, had to come more swiftly (in effect, it began with the "own funds" import programme in 1984), it came fairly *gradually* and slowly. By the mid-1990s, the economy had significantly recovered and donors had returned. Remarkably, political stability had been a constant.

By this time, however, Tanzania was in trouble over other issues. Corruption had reached the highest levels of the government and party (attracting public criticism from, among others, the now-retired Mwalimu, who now also supported competitive elections in a multi-party system); the central economic policymaking machinery was demoralised and in disarray; and, partly in consequence, aid donors were almost totally driving such development efforts as were under way (outside the private sector). Economic growth was taking place but there was a notable absence of any public vision, such as had characterised the Nyerere years, as to where the country was going and why. Economic policy was seen as dictated by the international financial institutions and the aid donors.[3]

The government of Benjamin Mkapa, newly elected in 1995, set out, with the encouragement of some of the major aid donors, to restore ownership of its own development programmes, fight corruption, and recreate a sense of vision of the country's direction. While much remains to be done, to a remarkable degree, it seems to me, it has been succeeding. It reached an important agreement, in principle, with the aid donor community on appropriate aid relationships — and, again, while much remains to be done, there can be no doubt that ownership of economic policy and programmes is returning to Tanzania. The government has prepared its own policy framework paper and its own long-term vision statement (both with non-governmental inputs), led its own public expenditure review and the new Tanzania Assistance Strategy, and will now develop its own Poverty Reduction Strategy Paper. Increasing (though still too small) proportions of aid expenditure are flowing through (or at least reported in) the national budget as the central economic administration strengthens. Tanzanian-led sectoral strategies and policies are being developed and implemented in health, roads and education. Prime emphasis throughout these efforts is to address the principal problems of poverty and to do so under Tanzanian, not donor, leadership.[4]

One senior (and informed) World Bank official has remarked to me privately that, despite all the favourable press on Uganda, Tanzania is actually about four years or more ahead of it in terms of truly nationally-owned (and thus sustainable) economic policy for overall development. Tanzania may seem to move more slowly he noted, and I agree, but it does so on a firmer and more stable base.

This base was established, I would argue, in the time of Julius Nyerere: a politically unified country; shared values as to equity in income distribution and political participation; and determination to develop and implement one's own policies and programmes. Because Tanzania now has in place all of the key elements for sustained development — macroeconomic stability; broadly sensible incentive structures; broad political participation and stability; growing national self-confidence, ownership and capacity — I believe it is likely that, barring calamities of weather or the terms of trade, Tanzania will soon be everyone's favourite African 'success story' (and model) once again.

It is now conventional wisdom in Washington (even in the IMF, at least in terms of its rhetoric), and in donor capitals, that poverty needs to be addressed as a matter of highest priority; that political stability and good governance (notably reduced corruption) are prerequisites for development; and that national ownership of programmes is critical to their success. It has taken them a long time to reach these positions. But Julius Nyerere was espousing them and trying to build practice upon them 30 years ago. His slogan of "socialism and self-reliance", if transmitted today as "equity, honesty and ownership", would win universal assent. He was decades ahead of his time in these matters.

Today's key Tanzanian policymakers — both politicians and technocrats — grew up and were educated in the Nyerere years. They have undoubtedly learned from earlier economic and other policy mistakes. Mwalimu was himself a learner and pragmatist, who often changed policy positions when the evidence as to the failure of previous approaches seemed clear. I believe that the respect which Mwalimu enjoyed in his own country right up until his death indicates that they also retained much that Mwalimu had taught. They now can build "humane governance" on the political and value base he constructed.[5]

Whatever his other mistakes in the realm of economics, in one area of economic policy Mwalimu was dead right — and, again, ahead of his time. Both in his anguished cry about the IMF in 1981 and in his subsequent work in the South Commission and the South Centre, he steadily maintained the need for fairer international (or global) systems of economic governance, particularly in the financial sphere. It is important to underline his consistent emphasis upon *equity* in global economic governance arrangements because there is every sign that current reform efforts in the international financial arena are overly focused upon efficiency considerations and the avoidance or minimisation of the effects of systemic crises. This focus has resulted in some effort to incorporate some of the interests and concerns of the newly emerging countries and the largest of the poor countries, and this certainly constitutes important progress in global economic and financial governance; but it leaves out the poorest and weakest. The latter are unrepresented, either in the new Financial Stability Forum or in the even newer Group of Twenty (G20), chaired by the Canadian Finance Minister. (The G20 has also contrived to exclude all of the so-called 'like-minded' countries, who might be expected to take a deeper interest in the problems of the poorest countries and peoples, as they have done in the past on debt relief and other issues.)

Nyerere's activities in the international/global sphere included efforts to bolster analysis, both economic and political, to inform those who speak for developing countries, especially the poorest among them, in international negotiations and organisations. Developing countries are still woefully under-equipped to deal with the batteries of well-funded economists, lawyers and lobbyists who defend Northern interests in international discussions and the media. He was among those who saw, far ahead of others, that there is ultimately no substitute for one's own technical, professional and institutional strength. Today it is known as 'capacity building', and it has entered conventional wisdom as to what is to be done not only in Africa but throughout the developing world.

Yes, Julius Nyerere made some economic policy mistakes. In this he was certainly not alone. He also left a country capable of learning from its experience with a minimum of political ruckus, a country now moving forward economically on a firm political and value base. That is a significant legacy. At the international level the fruits of his efforts are probably more distant. I expect, however, that one day they too will come.

Endnotes

1 My personal anxieties in this regard, circa 1969-70, may be found in an article in the *Journal of Development Studies* 8 (1).

2 *Eliminating World Poverty: A Challenge for the 21st Century, White Paper on International Development*, November 1997, p. 9.

3 For an account, see the Helleiner Report: Helleiner, Gerald K., Killick, Tony, Lipumba, Nguyuru, Ndulu, Benno J. and Svendsen, Knud Erik. *Report of the Group of Independent Advisers on Development Cooperation Issues Between Tanzania and Its Aid Donors.* Royal Danish Ministry of Foreign Affairs, June 1995.

4 More details on all this can be found in a paper prepared for the May 1999 meeting of the Consultative Group for Tanzania: Helleiner, Gerry. "Changing Aid Relationships in Tanzania, December 1997 through March 1999." Mimeo. Dar es Salaam, 1999.

5 The apt concept of "humane governance" has recently been developed to encompass sound and equitable economic *and* political governance, including responsive and participatory institutions, respect for human rights, and special provision for the most needy and most vulnerable. See ul Haq, Mahbub. *Human Development in South Asia, 1999.* Pakistan: The Human Development Centre and Oxford University Press, 1999.

CHAPTER SIX

Question and Answer Period

Following the panel presentations, Colin Leys summarized the key themes raised by the panelists and offered some of his own thoughts on the legacies of Nyerere. Leys' presentation is transcribed below, followed by a "question and answer" period from the floor. The chapter concludes with a round of responses from the panel. Unfortunately, we were only able to record a portion of the questions/comments from the floor. We were, however, able to record and transcribe all of the responses from the panel and these are presented here in the order that the panelists spoke.

Summary of Panel Discussion

Colin Leys:[1] It has been a pleasure to hear such a distinguished panel of authorities on this subject, and it has reminded me of what a privilege it was to have been in East Africa during Julius Nyerere's greatest years. As Gerry Helleiner has said, it was something to be young and to be in a country with an inspiring, young leader. We are also privileged to be taking part in one of the first occasions to pose retrospective questions about Africa's greatest modern philosopher king (he would not have liked the term 'king', of course, though he might have accepted 'philosopher').

We are celebrating Nyerere's legacy, but also trying to understand it. He himself would not be happy if we were only trying to celebrate it. What we are trying to do is, I think, what he would have expected of us: to apply to his thought and practice the same sympathetic scepticism that he himself brought to any set of ideas. In thinking about the balance to be struck between celebration and criticism I am reminded of a passage in one of Mao Zedong's speeches. This is not inappropriate because, of course, Nyerere was very influenced by an early visit he paid to China, before the decline of the Maoist leadership had set in. He was particularly struck by the apparent austerity of the Chinese leaders' lives. I think I am right in saying that the fashion for the famous 'Chou En Lai' coat that was adopted in East Africa and spread elsewhere in Africa stemmed from Nyerere's early visit to China and its influence also on some of the people who went with him. But besides this apparent austerity, Nyerere was also sympathetic to Mao's constant efforts to teach — something both men had in common as leaders — and to Mao's attitude to ideas — his view that ideas should be useful. For example Nyerere liked the passage in one of Mao's lectures when he told his own Central Committee: "How is Marxist-Leninist theory to be linked with the practice of the Chinese revolution? To use a common expression, it is by shooting the arrow at the target." Some people, he said, "merely stroke the arrow fondly, exclaiming 'What a fine arrow! What a fine arrow!', but never want to shoot it. These people are only connoisseurs of curios and have virtually nothing to do with the revolution. The arrow of Marxism-Leninism must be used to shoot at the Chinese revolution."[2]

Nyerere was no Marxist-Leninist but unlike some other African political philosophers he shared Mao's view of the role of theory; and in looking at his own ideas, we should keep this in mind. In looking at Nyerere's legacy, we are not just doing it for its own sake, to get a better take on his life and works in their context, but should be trying to learn lessons from what he attempted, and what he achieved and what he failed to do, that are applicable to real conditions, and not just in Africa, but even farther afield. And how many leaders, of any country, have left such a rich, complicated, sometimes ambivalent but always important legacy of ideas and practice in so many areas? If one thinks of the really great modern leaders of Africa, how many have left as much? We need go no further than Mandela, a towering giant of our time. In comparison, Mandela has not left anything like the philosophical or practical legacy of Nyerere. He did not have the opportunity in his lifetime to pursue the wide range of initiatives that Nyerere was able to pursue. His peculiar accomplishment was different. But the comparison is useful in reminding us what an extraordinary phenomenon Nyerere's legacy of theory and practice is.

I have tried to pull together the ideas presented thus far at this conference under four themes. The first is the question of leadership, the second is the question of language, the third is the question of socialism and the fourth is the issue of Nyerere as a Pan-African leader, or even as a thinker and actor of worldwide importance.

Under the first point, the example of leadership, he was, in Ngugi's phrase, a leader who needed no motorcade, who wanted no motorcade. That separates him from the leaders of most post-independence African countries, certainly down to the 1980s. Nyerere is unique in that way: to be a leader and to be modest; to be a leader who doesn't need protection from his own people; to be a leader who doesn't need the trappings of power in order to lead. Something of this leadership legacy is still at work due to the extraordinarily deep impact he made in his own country, testified to by the account of the funeral in the moving letter quoted by Cran Pratt, and the massive turnout at the evening session at the Asmara conference described by Ngugi. The fact that his name resonates with anybody who is interested, not just in Africa, but also in socialism and questions of language, history, ethics and public life, testifies to the importance of his leadership. And his name is known in spite of the fact that Nyerere did not promote himself. He was not theatrical. He didn't seek the big stage. He succeeded in conveying his ideas just by speaking, by writing, and by the force of his personality.

I was privileged as a very young man to go to Tanzania in 1961 just before he became prime minister. What struck me about him, very forcibly, was his charm. He had a very buoyant, gay personality that caught you up in his enthusiasm and disarmed any objections you had. His style of leadership did not depend at all on his being a big person, but just on being a very clever, charming, entertaining and persuasive person. He was very charismatic in the best sense of the word. You either have charisma or you don't, and he had it. Contemplating someone with charisma doesn't teach you a lot about leadership, perhaps, since charisma can't be acquired; but you learn a lot from thinking about Nyerere's impact, about the importance of the fact that his principles were in fact wedded to his charm.

Charm, simplicity, modesty, the ethical basis of politics and leadership, his Catholic ethics, his social-democratic training as a graduate student in Edinburgh under Alexander Gray — all these shine through all his writings. These elements are, further, closely linked with his perception of the need to rely on one's own social and cultural base — on the society of which you are part, and from which you absorb so many principles and values. He did not say one should be grounded in this base in an unchanging way — on the contrary, he constantly challenged traditional ideas — but that one must be grounded in it. So, there is self-reliance — but the self-reliance of the whole community, rather than just each individual, so it includes also *selflessness*. On the other hand, and in contradiction to any narrow traditionalism, there is inclusiveness, a rejection of racism, of ethnicity or 'ethnicism', and even a rejection of nation, as grounds for divisions between people.

Given this remarkable set of principles, this immense performance, the question we are confronted with is what were the limits to leadership of this kind, how far could it go? There was weakness in the democratic component of this leadership. This is not in any way an impertinent comment, at least certainly not by intention. It is to raise a question which progressive people have neglected. The left has been reluctant to acknowledge the importance of leadership, and yet very little has been accomplished without leadership, so the question is: "How can leadership be made democratic?" Some of the things that John Saul referred to mark some of the limits of Nyerere's conception of his role as a leader. It is better to be a teacher than to be a bully, but do we also not want to emancipate ourselves from our teachers too?

I think there are some very important lessons for any country to learn by contemplating the strengths and limitations of Nyerere's leadership role. Was his readiness to retire, to have a civil succession, a sufficient contribution to the ideal of democratic leaderhsip? His willingness to go certainly separates him from most of his contemporary African leaders. But what about his paternalism? Could he have been anything but paternalistic when he was dealing with a country that had not been allowed to inherit the world's accumulated knowledge and wisdom (including such political wisdom as it has accumulated) through a decent school and university system, a decent press, a decent radio service, a public library system? He was a teacher and he was trying to convey big ideas to a nation of people who needed to be spoken to in terms they could understand, and most of whom lacked the knowledge and experience to challenge or question him. In this situation it was surely difficult not to become slightly paternalistic, but it is a problem. Similar problems arise over the relationship of the party as an organisation to the wider society. Can we imagine progressive social change taking place anywhere without something like political parties? And yet can we really imagine parties without apparatuses, with an independent interest of their own, of the kind that, according to Andrew Coulson and others, led to the momentous decision in 1969 to close down and destroy the Ruvuma Development Association and everything that it stood for in the way of real self-help, real democracy?

So in evaluating Nyerere's conception of leadership we need to know more about how he understood the party, and what he thought the problems were in making it more of a real force with roots in civil society. Were the mistakes it made unavoidable? Was his technical solution to the problem of reconciling democracy with a single party of offering voters a choice between two candidates an intelligent and appropriate solution? Could there have been others? In Uganda Museveni tried other alternatives, aimed at the same problem: the open voting system for a start, and then the ban on political parties. We must acknowledge that the problem these leaders were confronting is real. If they had simply opened the electoral system up to rival parties, they would very likely have been based on ethnic, regional and/or religious bases, which would have made progressive government extremely difficult, if not impossible. The experience of African countries in multi-party systems since the 1990s shows that the problem is not readily disposed of by just adopting 'pluralism' in a formal institutional fashion.

I was very struck, finally, by Gerry Helleiner's observation today that the social base for what he sees as Tanzania's recent recovery, and its capacity to move forward in a self-reliant way, was laid in Nyerere's time. If that is true, there is a very important lesson there to be articulated and learned.

Now to the second theme of language. It is difficult for people who are not specialists in the field, and certainly in the presence of Ngugi, to take up this theme, but one should think about this broadly. If you ask any French-speaking person in Canada what it felt like before the Quiet Revolution to live one's life in a foreign language — i.e., English, again the language of a dominant colonial power — you will get a very similar answer to that of any African. What it is like, if your mother tongue is French or XXX, to have to live your life in English — or if it is XXX, to have to live it in French? There is no question that language is, for all the reasons that Ngugi outlined for us, fundamental, and the Asmara Declaration may become the turning-point that he is talking about. The politics of this are really problematic, however. Tanzania is interestingly different because there is an African *lingua franca*, which other countries on the whole don't have, in the shape of Kiswahili, so the many different languages that co-exist in Tanzania can be developed and respected and drawn upon at the same time as a common language is also developed, which is not the language of the colonialisers, and which is widely understood. I may have got this wrong, but it seems to me that there is an obvious tension between being for national unity, for transnational unity, for African continental unity, and yet knowing that you must let people develop politically and act within their own language because this embodies so much of their identity and the values that bind them together. There is a set of very interesting questions there we must hope Ngugi and others here will develop.

As for the third theme, socialism, what one saw dramatically in several of the conference presentations thus far were the tensions in Nyerere's thought between idealism and materialism, between ethics and structure. On the one hand there is the Roman Catholic ethic, blended with his powerful intuitive connection to the collective aspect of African traditional cultures. On the other hand there is the clarity of mind that allowed him to identify the threats to African development, African unity, African self-respect, presented by global capitalism, and the prescient way in which he described that. How far the mix was coherent is not yet entirely clear to me, and I doubt if history has pronounced a final verdict on it. In this connection, too, Gerry Helleiner again made an extremely interesting observation when he suggested that it wasn't the socialist policies of Nyerere that were responsible for Tanzania's economic decline in the 1980s, but poor macro-economic management, poor judgements about the exchange rate and related policies, which Tanzania made in common with many other African countries (and not just African countries). Unless this is a purely academic judgement it seems to imply that had these mistakes been avoided it would have been possible for Tanzania to pursue many of its socialist objectives, in spite of the hostility of the so-called international aid community. This is clearly a crucially important question, and if we can't solve it today, as we undoubtedly cannot, it is a very important research question for the future. How far was or is socialism in one country (or even in one continent) compatible with global capitalism, its so-called 'financial architecture' and its overall structure and balance of political forces? It seems to me that the answer to this may be illuminated by reviewing the history of Nyerere's Tanzania in light of the analysis that Gerry Helleiner is proposing.

Finally, I must limit myself here to simply identifying the fourth theme. Several of the presentations talked about the role of Nyerere as a regional and Pan-African leader. Let me simply say that there is evidently a need, first, to identify more of the elements of that role, and second, to evaluate it its achievements and its limitations. No doubt Nyerere's legacy in this area will provide substantial challenges to researchers for many years to come.

Questions and Comments from the Floor

Jonathan Barker:[3] There is an aspect of Nyerere's legacy that I think is vital and that has so far received little mention here: his emphasis on rural development and his vision (and his policy) of rural socialism. The dismissal across-the-board of his rural policies that is so frequent today is surely unjustified. In fact there is much to learn by looking at what seemed to work and what went wrong with *ujamaa vijijini* (village-level socialism). In my view there was a failure in political learning or political listening.

Nyerere's schoolmasterly side of knowing what was best for his charges came to the fore, rather than his commitment to the "two-way road" of communication that the party was supposed to become. My research in Tanzania with students from the University of Dar es Salaam in 1972 brought to light evidence that collective work in agricultural change has an important role in the establishment of new farms and villages, but that it cannot work in the long-run improvement of productivity among peasant-farmers of the kind found in Tanzania. It also suggested that there was at work a combination of ideological rigidity on the part of Nyerere himself and a political failure of the party and the administration in rural areas to communicate seriously and accurately the honest and reasoned resistance of farming people to collectivising control of land and agricultural work. Since the issue of agricultural change and improvement remains a critical issue for Tanzania and other African countries, the question of Tanzania's rural experiment is not one of merely historical interest. I would appreciate hearing some reflection on this issue.

Rohinton Medora:[4] Official development assistance (ODA) is about making choices. I put to the panel three propositions. First, the result of today's discussion has been that Nyerere's economic and political policies were mixed at best. There is ample evidence of sound ideas, personal rectitude, external shocks as well as authoritarianism, intervention in neighboring countries, corruption and inefficiency in the government. Second, there is a strong sense, conveyed recently — for example in the Dollar Report — that ODA should target countries that are well-run and have lots of poor people. Third, donor agencies face exigencies and must apply an often complex set of conditions to their aid which now go beyond the economic. This co-exists with an equally strong view among many development thinkers and practitioners that aid should be targeted with minimal micro-conditionality at countries that have chosen their own develop-ment paths and proven to implement these appropriately.

Bearing in mind the particular case of Tanzania, what reflections would you make on the relationship between Tanzania and its ODA partners?

Grif Cunningham:[5] At the time of independence in 1961 a 'brand new' country was created in Tanganyika. And indeed, much was new, perhaps more than in any other newly independent country. There was a new team of nation-builders placed in charge; a team of Tanganyikans, political leaders and civil servants replacing British colonial officials. And there were others, consisting of various foreign 'development experts', largely from friendly or like-minded countries like Canada.

The political system replacing the British colonial regime was also altogether new, with the country's first ever directly elected, very democratic, national gov-ernment. And in the regions and districts, a new cohort of Tanganyikans took over, with a lot to learn about nation-building and administration.

More important, perhaps, was the nation-building policy that gradually emerged as Julius Nyerere developed his "African Socialist" agenda. Within a few years of independence, Nyerere and his TANU colleagues had adopted a very ambitious and socialist development strategy for which Tanzania and Nyerere became quite famous.

Tanzania's brand of socialism was actually a significant presence from the time of independence, but was not so much foreground as background when devel-opment decisions were being made. Nyerere was not, it seems in the beginning, worried about this because of his often-stated belief that most Africans were fundamentally socialists. He meant by this that their culture or ethnicity, land-holding system and traditional economy were all quite naturally highly collec-tive or communal, hence socialist, or at least African socialist.

But the agencies available for actual socialist development were a bit of a prob-lem. The central government was always the principal centre of development activity. From the time of independence onwards, the role of government was in a constant state of expansion, though very often without an adequate increase in the availability and quality of resources, and very often without much concern for the socialist content of the development being considered. The two ministries mostly responsible for *ujamaa* village development in the late 1960s had only a handful of civil servants, not all of whom were enthusiastic supporters of a policy of socialist rural development in any form. I had experience in both ministries.

And what about TANU, the political party in charge? In theory, the Party consisted of a number of essential forces necessary for the building of a socialist state. In the Party, in Dar es Salaam and in the countryside, one might hope to find the cadre essential to the development of socialism in a, by then, one-party state. In the Party there should have been a vanguard ready, willing and able to promote and implement a socialist nation building policy that had been adopted by the Party at its various congresses.

Where might this vanguard or socialist cadre come from? Kivukoni College was obviously the training ground for some of this leadership, if not all of it. I was principal of the college for an important period of this socialist nation-building, and Julius Nyerere was always very much present as the founder, conscience, and inspiration of staff and students. The college's job was to provide training and education of a particular quality for socialist nation-building for Party leaders, for government officials, and a significant number of other mature adults with the potential to perform an appropriate leadership role somewhere in the country. Without a doubt we were a success and had a significant impact on the lives and careers of many of our students.

However, neither the government nor the Party was adequately resourced or sufficiently socialist-minded to perform the very radical tasks assigned to them. Government was hierarchical and tended to the authoritarian in the usual ways, and the Party was not really a significant player. Almost all the original Party leadership had been sucked into government in the early 1960s. And Kivukoni College was given the impossible task of developing a socialist cadre of nation-builders charged with the task of performing miracles.

The possible role of a Party-centered vanguard movement was a much debated issue among the Left intellectuals who gathered regularly at the University of Dar es Salaam in the 1960s. One such vanguard, the Ruvuma Development Association (RDA), was actually established and had a significant but brief existence in the Ruvuma Region in Southern Tanzania. During that time I was their active ally and resource person in Dar es Salaam. The success of the RDA may have been its undoing, because the policy of *ujamaa* village development was based, in part at least, on their success and that of other such collective enterprises. But vanguard movements were never popular in Tanzania, and when making such village collectives a national development policy, the Party promptly and forcefully shut down the RDA.

Tanzania's adoption of socialism as the nation-building ideology was a major event in post-independence African history. This commitment to a socialist course of development was almost entirely the result of Julius Nyerere's inspired and inspiring leadership. Implementing such an ambitious policy clearly needed the commitment and skilled labour of a small multitude, and, for various reasons, that multitude does not seem to have been available.

Dan O'Meara:[6] In an era of globalization, and when socialism as we know it has been seen to fail to deliver, what is it we mean by 'socialism' today? In my mind, any new egalitarian project must come up with a new name and a new set of mechanisms and objectives for what it is we want to achieve. I would like to ask the panel to comment on this point.

Marc Epprecht:[7] I would like to solicit comments upon two aspects of Nyerere's socialism and Pan-Africanism which the panelists have not yet addressed. First, we have heard a lot about Nyerere's truly impressive achievements as an African leader. Under his rule Tanzania pioneered such policies as an anti-corruption code for civil servants and politicians, solidarity with southern African libera-tion movements, the development of an indigenous language (Swahili) into a national language of governance and culture, land resettlement, democratic struc-tures of governance including establishing the principle of a leader's gracious retirement from office, and so on. In the face of so much 'Afro-pessimism' and cynicism about politics these days, how refreshing and exciting it is for me to be able to share in this reflection on the historical fact of a principled, courageous, and far-sighted African leader.

Nonetheless, I am a bit surprised that in all this talk of Tanzanian 'firsts' and moral leadership under Nyerere, no one has mentioned one particular first which, in retrospect, arguably had disastrous consequences not just for Tanzania but for the Great Lakes region in general. I am talking about his decision to invade Uganda in 1978 to overthrow Idi Amin. If I am not mistaken this was the first time one African nation openly violated the Organization of African Unity (OAU) principle of non-intervention in another. The invasion was successful in remov-ing Amin and stabilizing Tanzania's border area, although at onerous cost to Tanzanian citizens in general. The successor 'democratic' regime of Milton Obote that Nyerere helped usher back into power, however, quickly proved to be even worse than Amin's.

Retribution killings, ethnic discrimination, and naked pillage of economic resources reduced the country to a shambles and inflamed violent, and in some cases almost demented, millenial rebellions. Some scholars have even argued that the ripple effect of Obote's repression, particularly that which was directed against Tutsi refugees in southern Uganda, spilled over into Rwanda. In that way the Obote regime contributed to precipitating the genocide in Rwanda and beyond.

Obviously Nyerere can in no way be held responsible for the genocide. It seems, however, that his misguided loyalty to Obote does implicate him in both that tragedy and in the current 'African World War' engulfing the Congo. Could anyone explain to me how Nyerere could be so grievously wrong about the character of the man he bestowed to power in Uganda?

The second silence that worries me a bit is on the topic of gender. We have heard a lot about Nyerere's socialism and his determination to counter the legacies of class, race, and ethnic inequality left behind by racial capitalism and colonial rule. As Kenya at the time, and Tanzania since Nyerere left office, abundantly illustrate, global capitalism feeds upon and exacerbates those legacies as a normal — some even say desirable — part of the capitalist working day. That Nyerere took concrete steps to stymie emerging elitism and tribalism after independence and to redistribute scarce resources to the rural poor may therefore have depressed some conventional indicators of economic growth. However, they laid the basis for long-term, sustainable development. Notwithstanding the imposition of neo-liberal dogma since his departure from office, Nyerere's policies may in fact have left Tanzania with a comparative advantage over other African nations in terms of literacy, social justice and political stability that bodes well for future economic 'take-off'. How ironic (although of course with many historical precedents elsewhere) that the long-term interests of capitalists in Africa may be saved from their own short-term greed and stupidity by 'failed socialist policies'.

But socialism involves more than redressing class, ethnic and racial inequalities. Indeed, socialist revolution without a transformation in gender relations is demonstrably doomed to failure as 'bourgeois' family models and notions of sexuality constantly recreate other oppressive, hierarchical social relations. Some of Nyerere's contemporaries — Sekou Tour, Modibo Keita, Samora Machel, and Thomas Sankara, for example — recognised this quite explicitly. The emancipation of women from the patriarchal neo-traditions that had been cultivated during colonial rule was integral to their revolutionary platforms.

It seems to me that Nyerere was uncharacteristically quiet if not actively bourgeois on this issue. Certainly he was in favour of women's equality with men as citizens in a basically liberal feminist kind of way — give girls education and women legal rights and so on, and they will advance. But it does not seem that he was prepared to take the radical steps needed to guard against new, emergent forms of gender inequality and oppression. I do not want to overstate this but, for example, in the absence of explicit leadership against the practice, a revival of female genital mutilation has been taking place. Girls hope to catch husbands by appealing to idealised traditions which put their health and, arguably, their humanity at considerable risk. The Tanzanian state, like many other African nations, has also been reluctant to take an explicit leadership role in the fight against sexually transmitted diseases, HIV/AIDS above all.

Could any of the presenters comment on Nyerere's understanding of the role of gender in socialist development? I am particularly interested to learn whether his attitudes toward sexuality may have unintentionally inhibited women's (and men's) emancipation from oppressive and unhealthy gender roles.

David McDonald: I would like to take up the theme of self-reliance as it was seen by Nyerere and ask the panel what they think it means in today's world of ever-increasing corporate globalisation. Are we talking here of some kind of 'constructive engagement' with the world economy on the part of African nations, or is this, as Samir Amin has argued, and as some of you this morning have suggested, an impossible dream, requiring a much more radical vision of 'delinking' African nations from the world economy? If the latter, what does this imply for regional and/or Pan-African relations in terms of trade and other forms of interstate exchange (culture, migration, and so on)? Finally, is there a leader in Africa today (and is a 'leader' in fact what is required) who can make this kind of delinking a practical reality?

Responses from the Panel

Ngugi wa Thiong'o: I would like to respond to the question about 'delinking' — whether it is possible for Africa to delink from the global capitalist system. My own quick response is that it is not possible to delink. The question really is what kind of linkages we need to have. That is the question that we need to be posing.

When you look at the development of capitalism the global element has always been there: with the explorations of the so-called new worlds; with the first exportation of labour by way of slave trading; and so on. When it comes to the industrial, capitalist phase, again that has a global dimension with the new colonial systems in Africa and elsewhere. Remember the first phase of capital expansion results in, literally, communities being made to fight against each other, slavery, slaves and so on. With the second phase you get colonies *within* Africa; again, the same kind of divisions of the major colonial powers. In all cases, it is really a question of division. Then we come to the finance capitalist phase, which is the more complicated. You can divide this phase into two, actually, the first happening during or just preceding the Cold War and the second happening since end of the Cold War. You can see that in the Cold War era, when Nyerere and others come into being, financial capital takes advantage of the colonial system (which is itself a product of globalisation). We quite clearly had active support of dictatorships within Africa by financial capital. It does not really matter what systems they develop as long as there were actually dictators walking in conjunction with the West in all those countries. It is very interesting, that the so-called Bretton Woods institutions come into being at the end of the Second World War in 1946.

Then there is the post–Cold War state of finance. There is what I would call 'capitalist fundamentalism' at work. Finance capital has to be free to move across state barriers, while at the same time, there is an erection of barriers to the movement of labour. This results in the creation of very weak states. Too weak to put any kind of resistance to the movement of finance capital, but strong enough to suppress populations should they want to do something about what is happening to them. This also brings in the question of non-governmental organisations, who become now the secular missionary counterparts of the religious missionaries of the nineteenth century, and they operate in much the same way. So, it is not a question of destroying the states in Africa or weakening them, but rather asking the same old question: whose state and what kind of state? The question of unity, of democracy, again comes in, because I would go for a state which is controlled in some way by the people. And for people to be able to control the state there has to be empowerment. With empowerment, there has to be democracy, there has to be unity, and so on. The question of languages, with which to understand what is happening, then comes into the picture.

There was also a question posed about language and unity, particularly the issue of *many* languages and unity. There is a way in which we can use even the linguistic divisions of Africa to our advantage. Take, for instance, the Ethiopia/ Eritrea conflict. The fact is they share communities on either side who speak the same language. Instead of seeing colonial boundaries as being sacrosanct we can use what I am calling shared communities. Between Kenya and Tanzania we have Masai people on both sides. There is no reason why we cannot use the fact that we share Masai people on both sides as the basis for trying to unify Kenya and Tanzania. If we do that, we can see that in fact there is both a linguistic and cultural chain, or linkages, of unity across the entire continent.

John Saul: A number of useful issues have been raised. I'm glad that Dan O'Meara brought the discussion back to an evaluation of the leadership code, for example. And I think even more could be said about Nyerere's links to the Southern African liberation struggle. Here, as elsewhere, it is not only his deep commitment to the success of nationalist assertions throughout the region that is on display but also other aspects of his intellectual formation, notably his Catholicism and (for want of a better term) his Fabianism, things that sometimes made his approach to movements like the African National Congress (ANC), with its communists links, an unduly wary (if nonetheless largely supportive) one. In this way, as with the discussion of his domestic political practice, we are forced to deepen our understanding of the diverse and sometimes seemingly contradictory intellectual strands that shaped his own specific (and occasionally contradictory!) left-of-centre perspective.

An equally revealing aspect of his southern African practice was the kind of commitment to "benign authoritarianism" suggested by his key role in supporting the "Presidential Club" of liberation movement leaders (a notion that I introduced this morning, most notably with reference to Nyerere's dubious interventions to save the SWAPO leadership-in-exile from the embarrassment of democratic pressures from within their own movement). Here, too, there are important clues for deepening our discussion of the strengths and weaknesses of his left-nationalist project within Tanzania itself.

But let me respond to the preceding discussion by focusing principally on the two particular aspects of the Nyerere project that have been raised most centrally for debate here, the issue of the political base (and of democratic practice with reference to it) for Nyerere's socialist endeavours and the issue — epitomised by David McDonald's evocation of the concept of 'delinking' — of Nyerere's economic stance towards the global economy. Consider, first, the question of the base, or, more clearly put, the issues raised by examining the politics of attempting to mobilise a popular base behind Nyerere's radical initiatives. Obviously it is important to take note, as we have done here, of the interesting ways in which Nyerere acted — the leadership code is a good example — to weaken the purchase on policymaking of those that sought to oppose the kind of left project he had in mind. And yet it is crucially important to remind ourselves that Nyerere didn't just act to neutralize those who didn't quite 'get it', those who didn't understand what he was trying to do or else chose for their own reasons to actually impede his policies. For Nyerere also acted assertively against some who did in fact 'get it', some who were committed to radical change but not quite in the way Nyerere himself thought that change should be construed and implemented.

My sense is that the costs to the cause of socialist endeavour in Tanzania, of the undemocratic propensities revealed by Nyerere's actions towards the latter, were high. This is why I chose in my talk to emphasise things like his confrontations with students and faculty at the University and his obvious discomfort, in the end, with the Ruvuma Development Association (RDA) (if we are not to believe of the latter incident, as I insist we should not, that he was merely railroaded into an authoritarian stance on the issue by right-wing regional commissioners). Here, too, one thinks of the cogent, but essentially limited way, in which Nyerere narrowed the debate about democracy to a choice between, on the one hand, the "democratic one-party state" option that he favoured and, on the other, a multiparty system. For even if you believed, as Nyerere apparently did, that the one-party system offered more space for people to empower themselves than in fact it proved to have in practice, you would still have to face more seriously than Nyerere ever did the fact that workers had no organisations in 'democratic' Tanzania that allowed them really to ground and express their interests, that women had no really independent organisations that would allow them to develop and express their interests, and that peasants, when they stepped outside the mainstream of Tanzanian debate on the issues that really concerned them (as they did through the RDA), got smashed. True, the RDA experiment took place in only one small corner of Tanzania and perhaps we should be careful of overstating the significance of its defeat. Still, I think the significance of the RDA's moment in Tanzanian history can even more easily be understated.

For the RDA symbolised an alternative way of developing socialism in Tanzania from below, and a way that was potentially much more meaningful and promising than any either permitted or encouraged by Nyerere. Nor is this to fall back on some romantic notion of the peasantry rising up spontaneously to create rural socialism. Leadership would have been required, but there would also have had to be a much more confident sense of give-and-take between leadership and mass activism than Nyerere's TANU was ever capable of risking in practice. Perhaps this is what Grif Cunningham was seeking to argue in his own earlier comment, although he tended to stress the fact that, in any case, TANU was just too weak an organisation to do what it was being instructed to do (i.e., to run the whole show and make *ujamaa* work!). But is it not even more important to make another kind of argument: whatever the level of TANU's 'effectiveness', what was really required was a very different method of political work and a very different horizon of political possibility than Nyerere and TANU could imagine. For only if these latter had been on offer might an enthusiastic embrace of the struggle to realise an alternative development path have been evoked from the people — whether in the workplace, the women's organisations, or the villages. Moreover, it was precisely Nyerere's failure of imagination in this sphere, his failure to learn from the RDA, that would ultimately lead to the disastrous nationwide policy of enforced villagization. In sum, the unresolved issue of how to establish a more effective and more genuinely democratic dialectic between leadership and base in the process of struggling for progressive outcomes must remain central to any ongoing discussion of Nyerere's project.

As anticipated above, the second issue I want to refer to is that of 'delinking'. This is a critical issue but it is one not easy to discuss briefly since it implicates the very large question of just what each of us thinks might have to be done in order to actually free up Africa for some kind of developmental transformation. If, on the one hand, you believe that the global (capitalist) system as it currently operates, does not provide the space for the sort of accumulation of capital and transformation of economic and social possibility that Africa generally, and Tanzania more specifically, requires then you are led to ask a set of quite radical questions and envisage the necessity of a quite radical set of policies. If, on the other hand, you don't feel this way about the global system (or even if you think that, whatever its demerits, that system is not about to change and therefore "There Is No Alternative" but to conform to it) then you ask another set of questions and come to define a much more modest set of policies. You then start figuring out ways to more effectively manoeuvre within that system in order to make the lives of the people somewhat better (or, as has more often been the case in Africa, to manoeuvre within it as leaders merely to meet your own much more narrow class interests).

Here, too, we enter the land of *déjà vu*. For Gerry Helleiner and I have been having the same argument about this issue — reform versus revolution — ever since our days together in Tanzania in the 1960s. Of course, I don't know enough about contemporary Tanzania to argue with Gerry substantively about the strength and weaknesses of Tanzania's current policies, policies that he has praised here today. But I do continue to question his premises. For it seems to me that the post-Nyerere Tanzania Gerry has presented as a 'new model for transformation' in Africa is a Tanzania that has accepted, by and large, the dictate of global capitalism. And the fact remains that the IMF and World Bank have not really changed their tune even if, within their framework (but perhaps also on the basis of the high level of national unity that Nyerere helped to build), Tanzania has indeed been able to discover a less corrupt and more effective way of 'working the margins' of the global system. Is this, then, a post-Nyerere success story?

Unfortunately, I suspect that to the extent the present outcome appears to be so it is merely because we now take as 'common-sense' a much diminished level of expectation about what ordinary people can expect to achieve in their own lives in terms of development. In short, such an approach helps further to rationalise an ever greater marginalisation of the vast mass of the population in African countries, not least in Tanzania.

At best, then, what we see is a 'renaissance' for a few people who now get richer, but something that is very far from being a renaissance for those further down the social hierarchy.

So, 'good governance'? Well yes, where it is achieved it is better than having civil wars and completely corrupt states. But this and other currently fashionable 'accomplishments' are framed by such a narrow set of possibilities within the overarching workings of a malignant global capitalism that they are not really such very great accomplishments after all. For they must be set against a much more central problem: a worldwide economic system that is fundamentally biased against the realisation of opportunities for the vast majority of Africans. If that system is here to stay, heaven help us. True, it may appear to be 'realistic' to accept that framework and to merely work for the most humane outcomes within it. It is perhaps too easy for me to say the contrary, living, as I do, at such a distance from the African front line of the war against poverty and exploitation. Fortunate, then, that it is precisely at this point that we can evoke Nyerere's own example. For whatever else we might choose to say about the various strengths and weaknesses of his diverse project he did consistently refuse any such 'realism' about the nature of the world system and about Africa's place within it: "It is broke and we MUST fix it," he seemed to say. He was, in short, amongst those in

Africa who encouraged us to think long and hard about large and very tough choices and about the indefensible nature of the broader socio-economic frameworks within which Africans are forced to make such narrow choices about what they can 'realistically' expect to attain. This was Nyerere's great strength and it stands in sharp contrast to the fast-sinking level of expectations — and the distinct failure of nerve — with which too many now view the continent and its prospects.

Julius Nyang'oro: I would like to make one comment based on the commentary on South Africa and the comparison between what has happened to the African National Congress and what they could learn from Julius Nyerere. Clearly, of course, the ANC has not learned from Julius Nyerere, and reading between the lines I think, going back to that speech that I referred to earlier, there is a warning from him. He was telling the South Africans, "Don't think that you are so special, because if you are used as a conduit for international capital to simply come and destroy the rest of the continent, you, yourselves are not going to become better. If anything, after capitalists are finished with you, you will be probably worse off than we are." In many ways, this is also the response to the question, what is the regional base upon which you can build a structure by which most of Africans liberate themselves from the ravages of poverty and other kinds of ills. To me, what was destructive about the film that we just watched [on *ujaama* villages] was the reality of poverty and difficult life. Whichever way you look at it, that is an extremely hard life. If you are president of a country and 95% of the population in your country live the way we saw on the film then we are dealing with big issues.

What do you do as a leader? We have such a huge task in front of us in Tanzania. Here we are, bickering over 4,000 shillings in Dar es Salaam, when 4,000 shillings is able to feed twenty villages, for two to three years. Why don't we get it? Because if we get it then we would understand why it is so important that we move on, not only from not wanting high salaries, but also from the need to create a one-party state because it creates unity that does not create the problems that have affected other countries.

I want to read a paragraph from something that Nyerere wrote in 1995 called "Our Leadership and the Destiny of Tanzania". This was his reaction to the creation of a multi-party political system in Tanzania, basically justifying on the one hand why it was important for there to be a one-party system before 1991-1992. He says:

It is very illogical to argue that moving to a multi-party system is to make the country more democratic and at the same time to deny the right to stand for elective office to any citizen who decides to join a political party, or to stand against his party's official candidate. At this point let me make it clear that I am not denying that this right for every citizen to stand in an election was effectively denied during the one-party system. I argued then, and I argue now, that when that system was introduced and the one-party system as it operated in this country with two candidates from the one party being submitted to their choice of all citizens, was the most democratic and most appropriate system under the circumstances of that time. By deciding to move to a multi-party system, which I support, we are saying that the circumstances have changed. Therefore, friction on the exercise of one of the people's basic rights can be lifted without endangering the unity and peace of this country, provided that they don't use race, tribe or religion as the basis for their appeals to the electorate.

What this illustrates to me, is the ability and capacity of Julius Nyerere to learn from past mistakes. It also helps me understand the frustration by which his practice becomes undemocratic.

Cranford Pratt: I would like briefly to underline the significance of Nyerere's diagnosis of a central domestic problem which Tanzania faced and which he felt to be of central importance. He recognised that Tanzania, and by implication many other African states, were very poor and were going to remain poor for a very long time, however successful they might be in their promotion of development. In such circumstances, the distribution of the results of whatever growth is generated becomes centrally important to the welfare of the people and to the social tranquility and unity of society. It would be unwise to rely on long-term growth to eventually bring improvements to the lot of the poor.

Nyerere was first among African leaders to recognise that the members of the political and bureaucratic elites in the newly independent states of Africa were very likely to put their own personal accumulation of wealth ahead of the promotion of the development of their own society. He deplored this emerging trend. It not only betrayed the high expectations that accompanied the achievement of independence but, for Nyerere in particular, it undermined indigenous egalitarian social values that he greatly treasured and which he was determined to preserve. Nyerere saw that deeper class divisions and a widening gap between the African elite and the African masses were already becoming a reality. That realisation explains the enormously rapid and radical set of socialist initiatives that he launched in 1967. He judged that if this process was not soon reversed, the deepening class stratification of Tanzania would become so entrenched that it would be irreversible.

Central to Nyerere's endeavour to ensure that Tanzania might achieve development while also retaining in modern form these traditional social values, were the twin projects to restructure Tanzanian rural society around *ujaama* villages and to devote the full leadership potential of the nationalist party, the Tanzanian African National Union (TANU), to the rapid development of communal cultivation of all commercial crops. Together, he hoped these profound changes would lead Tanzanians into a pattern of development that would establish modes of production and a style of life that would ensure that the social values of rural Tanzania would remain closely communal and egalitarian.

These socialist initiatives were attempted in circumstances that were, in important ways, favourable to their success. In 1967, Nyerere's prestige in Tanzania was still remarkably high, TANU was almost universally supported, there was little corruption within the public service, there were not yet severe class differentials, and older traditional communal values still commanded widespread respect. Yet as my opening comments suggested, Nyerere and TANU's efforts to promote the villagization of rural Tanzania and a socialist mode of agricultural production very substantially failed.

Grif Cunningham has forcefully identified as one important cause of this failure the fact that these socialist initiatives placed on the Party a task that was far beyond its managerial capacity. Traditional values in the countryside may well have been egalitarian but living in villages and farming collectively were profoundly counter to long-established practices. The hope was that TANU could capitalise on its undoubted popularity and lead Tanzanian farmers in their millions to embrace these profound changes in their way of life. As Grif has made clear it was a task vastly beyond the resources and skills of TANU.

There were two other aspects of this failure of the Party that I think must be factored in. Nyerere had relied on popular power expressed through the Party to maintain the integrity and responsibility of both the political and bureaucratic elites. TANU failed to be such a party. The representative institutions of TANU failed to give voice to the undoubted and widespread peasant hostility to being forced into villages and to being cajoled and bullied into experimenting with collective farming. By the middle of the 1970s, as I understand it, TANU had become dominated by its own bureaucracy. Its members, in their concern to advance their own self-interests, sought to please the president by supporting rather than challenging the socialist initiatives that they recognised he so strongly advocated and by blocking any articulation in TANU conferences of peasant opposition to these initiatives. It is often noted that powerful and popular leaders lead lonely lives, isolated from their own society by ambitious self-seekers and sycophants and ignorant of even important tides of opinion within their own societies. Nyerere by the late 1970s was an illustration of this political homily.

David McDonald asks what lessons of relevance to contemporary Africa can be learned from the Tanzanian effort to accomplish a socialist transformation of Tanzanian society. Let me suggest these two. First, it is crucially important to achieve and to sustain popular structures that will fearlessly articulate popular needs and wishes and democratic institutions capable of ensuring that those in power are answerable for their exercise of power. Neither charisma, personal character nor ideology is sufficient to ensure that power is not abused and the poor ignored. Tanzania has learned this truth the hard way. Even the integrity and honesty of Nyerere did not finally protect Tanzania from serious policy errors and a gradually increasing abuse of power by its political and bureaucratic elites. Fortunately this truth is increasingly recognised throughout Africa.

The second lesson that can perhaps be learned from the socialist experiment in Tanzania is that it is dangerous to ignore the accumulated wisdom of African farmers. In retrospect it seems clear that the lure of modern ways, ideology and a faith in education, generated in Tanzania a remarkable lack of respect for the judgement of African peasants about how farming is best done in Tanzania and about where peasants should be permitted to live and build their huts. I say "remarkable lack of respect" for this occurred despite Nyerere's profound commitment to the communal and egalitarian values of traditional Africa. This disrespect for the wisdom of African farmers is surely an important key to the understanding of why the *ujaama* villages and socialist farming failed in Tanzania. This position is argued brilliantly by James Scott in his recent and important book, *Seeing Like a State: How Certain Schemes to Improve the Human Condition Failed*. He persuasively argues that faith in high-modernist, centrally managed schemes to improve the human lot, combined with a disregard for local customs and practical knowledge, have been central to the failure of a number of major efforts to transform from above the lives of the poor. One of his key examples is the compulsory villagization in Tanzania in the 1970s.

Gerry Helleiner: There are so many critical questions and such rich discussion of them that it is difficult to know where to jump in. Let me confine my comments to a couple of points that were made. Firstly, with reference to the point about the leadership code and the comparison to the ANC, one has to be careful about this. There is a dilemma. I admired, and admire respectively, the leadership code introduced in Tanzania, but the fact is, that in the absence of adequate remuneration, highly skilled people migrate. That is not just in South Africa. That is a universal. There is an enormous, skilled African Diaspora now. It is easy enough to say that people should not be corrupt and that government should be transparent, and that there should be more appropriate ways in which bureaucrats behave, but when it comes to actually setting salaries the comparisons have to be made not simply with the private sector in South Africa, but with the world salary structure and that really does create a dilemma.

I don't have an answer. What I observe, and on a personal note, in looking at about 25 different African countries grappling with this and grappling with civil service salary reform issues and efforts to adequately reward those they want to keep or to attract back to their country I observe enormous variety from country to country in what the authorities or the knowledgeable people in the country believe to be necessary to bring people back. In some instances, it is said that you don't really require that much because, and Tanzania is one of these countries, because there is a sense of what it is that Nyerere built. There is a certain loyalty to the country which is greater in Tanzania than in many other countries that have been riddled by civil war, where it is downright dangerous to return, and where the salaries required to induce people to come and work in the president's office are of the level of the salaries of vice-presidents of the World Bank. Whatever it does for the domestic income distribution, they simply will not come unless you provide them with what I guess they would view as life insurance for their families. That is a dilemma, and so salary structure, as distinct from sheer corruption and malfeasance, is enormously complex.

Aid donors have not helped in this respect because in those countries that, for one reason or another, have not paid high salaries to their high-level people, aid donors have come in unasked (always unasked) and topped up their salaries directly. It does not go through any budget, it comes directly out of the aid donor's budget to the project, or the individual, who it is believed would otherwise leave the project or the country. That has, of course, bedeviled the efforts of salary reformers, whatever they are trying to do, to get their own structures right. This is a very complex question — I just wanted to signal that before one makes overly hasty inter-country comparisons.

The other point I want to address, and John says we have been arguing about this for 30 years, relates to this question of the relationship with the international system, the potential for delinking (if any), and whether there is a 'dumbing-down' of expectations in Africa and an acceptance of marginalisation as John aptly put it.

I believe that the global system is capable of some change. I don't believe that it will happen quickly. I do think that there are opportunities for pressure from people like us in the North to push Northern countries, governments and business corporations in the desirable directions, but when all is said and done, in the short to medium run, you cannot expect a great deal of change. That leaves Africans with not as much global space as I would like, but they have some. The advice that they receive, typically from the Bretton Woods institutions, has not been helpful because they are typically confronted with a dichotomous choice. The managing director of the IMF and the president of the World Bank and the head of the World Trade Organization are fond of making speeches about Africa in which they say, "You are being marginalised and your problem is that you are not integrating into the globalising world. Get on the train because it is moving and if you don't, you are going to be left behind." As if it was a yes or no question: Get on or not. And when they say get on, they mean get on in the way in which we are telling you to get on, which is in fact totally liberalising everything — open all doors to all manner of foreign inputs with limited degree of control. It is lying back in a mindless fashion and allowing yourself to be globalised. That is the advice — do this or don't do this and you are foolish if you don't. That is a very unhelpful way of proceeding.

One should view the global economy functionally. One should analyse as best one can, to see what one can get out of it and then construct one's policies in such a way as to get what one can out of it in the way that many East Asian countries did, relatively successfully. Some, now in Latin America as well, are not perfect societies. Don't misunderstand me, but they have achieved remarkable things with all kinds of controls and interventions, which may or not be described as socialist with different degrees of private capital involvement and interaction with the state. There have been agricultural revolutions in Indonesia. There has been a state-owned banking system in Taiwan from start to finish. I don't know why no one ever mentions that. There are a variety of ways of proceeding and what one requires for each case is undoubtedly different and it is not so easy to figure out exactly what it is. When there is some space I think it is possible to grow at the rate at which other countries, who began at the levels of which Africa now finds itself, did in the not too distant past — I am an Afro-optimist in that respect — but this will not happen if the African policymakers simply allow themselves mindless globalisation under the advice and pressure of foreign actors whose interests are directly involved.

So, lower expectations? I don't really think so among the African technocrats and technopols that I know. Is there a possibility for better international support? Now we come to Rohinton's point — absolutely, because the behaviour of donors (I know it best in Tanzania) has been reprehensible in all sorts of dimensions. Something like 30% of the total aid budget to Tanzania — that's higher than the rest of Africa — has been spent on technical assistance. Now, if those same funds had been deployed to back an appropriate civil service salary reform, to keep local consultants and to keep local people at home, that might have been a much more constructive use of the funds.

The most sensitive single issue, I believe, between African governments and the rest of the world in the aid community is technical assistance, which is deployed in ways in which African governments and peoples frequently don't want. They don't ask for it, it is a requirement, a condition, and a lot of it in the Tanzanian case (over 70% of the total budget, including the technical assistance) was never reported by the government, or went anywhere near a government budget. It went directly into individual pockets of consultants, foreign and local, directly into topping up the salaries, directly into NGO or local government activities, which the central government knew absolutely nothing about. Planning in those circumstances, when a very high proportion of the total budget is at present financed from outside, is impossible. Until that is sorted out (and I believe it is in the process of being sorted out, with great difficulty, because there are all kinds of donor interests and donor constraints that make it difficult), I think nothing much will happen.

There is a great deal more that could be said on all sorts of things and I have already gone over Colin's five-minute limit. Let me thank you for your very helpful and constructive comments and questions. I dare say, we will debate these issues again — those of us who are still alive in another twenty years.

Endnotes

1 Emeritus Professor of Political Studies at Queen's University, Kingston, Canada. Leys previously taught at the Universities of Oxford, Makerere (Uganda), Nairobi, Sussex and Sheffield and is a Fellow of the Royal Society of Canada.

2 "Rectify the Party's Style of Work", *Selected Works of Mao Tse-Tung.* (Peking: Foreign Languages Press, 1965, p. 42.

3 Professor Emeritus, Department of Political Science, University of Toronto, Canada.

4 Director, Social and Economic Equity Program and Partnership Branch, International Development Research Centre (IDRC), Ottawa, Canada.

5 Staff and then Principal of Kivukoni College, 1961-69; special assistant to President Nyerere on *ujamaa* village development, 1969-71; retired professor of Social Sciences, York University, Canada.

6 Professeur titulaire, Département de science politique, Université du Québec à Montréal.

7 Assistant Professor, Departments of History and Development Studies, Queen's University, Kingston, Canada.

CHAPTER SEVEN

Julius Nyerere's Critical Education Thought

Eunice Njeri Sahle

The central role of education in shaping the evolution of socio-political and economic systems in peripheral countries has been a recurring theme in development discourse and practice. This paper examines Julius Nyerere's ideas on the role of education in Tanzania's development and shows their relevance to development discourse. The paper has three parts: part one provides a brief account of the nature of the colonial education system; part two examines the main elements of Nyerere's critical education thought and examples of its practice; and the last part situates his ideas on education within the critical education theory tradition in an effort to demonstrate his enduring intellectual legacy.

Colonial Education

On the eve of independence Tanzania, like other colonies, inherited an education system that could not serve the needs and aspirations of an independent society. This was not an accident but a result of a deliberate colonial education policy that was geared to servicing the interests of the colonial state and the social forces closely linked to it. This process began with the establishment of Western formal schools by the missionaries and was consolidated during the evolution of colonial rule.

The history of formal education in Tanzania dates back to 1862 when the Holy Ghost Fathers established the first school at Bagamoyo. Other Christian missionaries such as the Lutheran Mission of Berlin and the Universities Mission to Central Africa followed suit. With the establishment of official colonial rule these two actors who were to shape the country's education sector were in place. The goals of the missionary schools were to bring 'civilization' to the so-called natives by introducing them to Christianity and basic literacy skills. For the colonial administration the objectives of its education policy was geared to serving the needs of the emerging capitalist economic system.

While stressing different goals, the missionaries and the colonial state's education objectives converged and hence reinforced the ethos of colonial political economy at the expense of those of the local African population. While Africans did have the opportunity to obtain formal education, a factor that played a major role in the rise of the nationalist movement, their numbers were insignificant and the content of colonial education was not geared to the needs of the local society. Thus, notwithstanding the declarations of the missionaries and liberal colonial administrators of their commitment to the advancement of Africans in Tanganyika a quick glance at the statistical evidence shows a grim picture with respect to education for Africans during the colonial era. According to David R. Morrison, in 1956:

> Only a minority of [African] children attended school: the enrollment in Standards I to IV of 336,000—a threefold increase over the previous decade—represented a mere thirty-nine per cent of children in the age-group from seven to eleven years. Of the pupils in Standard IV, one in seven entered Standard V; of those in Standard VII, one in four was placed in Standard IX. In 1952, 548 students had entered the first year of secondary school; only forty reached Makerere College in 1956....In contrast, European and Asian

children…had extensive educational facilities for their number…throughout the colonial period the number of places (in Tanganyika and elsewhere) corresponded roughly to the school-age population in the European community and to the demand for them in the Asian community…The relative advantage of non-Africans is strikingly illustrated in the fact that more Asians than Africans were enrolled in Standards IX to XII in 1956 despite a population ratio of Asians to Africans of less than 1:100.[1]

As Walter Rodney has argued, in Tanganyika the aim of the colonial regime was to have "a small section of the African population trained to fill various posts in the lower ranks of the administration, and to give, in turn, rudimentary instruction to their younger brothers in the primary schools. Consequently it was a system designed to buttress the status quo, which meant for the Africans economic exploitation, social inferiority and political dependence."[2] In broad terms the colonial education system was paternalist and racist in nature, features that left an indelible mark that would influence postcolonial developments in Tanzania and elsewhere in Africa. In the political sphere for instance, and as Agrippah T. Mugomba has persuasively argued, "there is a direct correlation between education for dependence and servitude, which the colonial school system overly emphasized, on the one hand, and the emergence of neocolonialism resulting in continuing dependency and underdevelopment, on the other." [3]

Nyerere's Critical Education Thought and Practice

At independence in 1961, Nyerere's regime embarked on a path geared to addressing the inadequacies of the colonial education system. Reforms were introduced that resulted, among others things, in the elimination of racial segregation in the school system, the expansion of the schools especially at the primary level and investment in the training of teachers. Despite these changes, the weaknesses of the inherited colonial education system manifested itself in various ways given the underlying economic structure of neocolonial peripheral capitalism and the ideological outlook of members of the ruling class. For instance, the expansion of the primary education system resulted in a crisis commonly referred to as the 'problem of primary school leavers'. As Rodney has argued, with political independence the ruling class had:

aimed to educate the maximum number of people and give them jobs in the modern sector. They had assumed the mantle of the colonial state and were prepared to carry out tasks which capitalism in the colonial era had failed to fulfil. But they were to find that capitalism in the postcolonial era was equally barren. The capitalist ethic was proving incompatible with the ideal of service to the community, while international capitalism was not permitting the Tanzanian economy to expand fast enough to meet the aspirations of those who completed their education at the primary level.[4]

Within the first five years of independence the contradictions of the inherited postcolonial political economic structure and Nyerere's commitment to the reorientation of the country's development path along what he termed "African socialism" saw him calling for radical changes in the education system. The central tenets of Nyerere's perspective on the role of education in the development process were contained in a 1967 policy booklet titled *Education for Self-Reliance*.[5] In this text Nyerere not only outlined his education philosophy but also provided a major critique of the education system that Tanzania inherited on the eve of independence. For Nyerere, this system had the following problems. To begin with, the colonial education served the needs of the metropolis and not those of Tanzanian society at large as evidenced by the limited number of educated Africans at independence. It was also designed in the hopes of changing local values and replacing them with the "knowledge from a different society."[6] In addition, the inherited system was elitist and not geared to meeting the needs of the majority of the citizens.[7] Further, it played a central role in the creation of a class-based society and generated "among those who succeed a feeling of superiority, and [left] the majority of the others hankering after something they will never obtain" and was thus an obstacle to the creation of "the egalitarian society we should build...[and] the attitudes of mind which are conducive to an egalitarian society."[8]

According to Nyerere the colonial education system separated students from their society thus creating a serious gap in their understanding of their own communities.[9] For instance, at the secondary school level most students were boarders and thus were separated from the struggles of their society for a long period of time.[10] In his view the inherited system had generated the notion that a school was "a place children go and which they and their parents hope will make it unnecessary for them to become farmers and continue living in the villages."[11] For Nyerere such an approach to education was out of place in a country were the majority of the population lived in the rural areas and was dependent on agrarian production.

Given the incompatibility of the inherited education system with the development goals of a peripheral country such as Tanzania, Nyerere contended that the time had come for Tanzanians to ask: "What is the educational system in Tanzania intend[ed] to do—what is its purpose?"[12] In his view the new education system was to have the following features. One, in order to meet the development goals set out in *The Arusha Declaration* it was to encourage co-operation in all areas of life and uphold the ideas of equality and community service.[13] Two, its core aim was to prepare young people for future contribution to their society, which was a rural one and highly dependent on agricultural production for its development. Three, it had to encourage the emergence of free citizens who could play a critical role in the evolution of the country's political economy. In this respect the education system was to "encourage the development in each citizen three things: an enquiring mind; an ability to learn from what others do, and reject or adapt it to his own needs; and a basic confidence in his own position as a free and equal member of the society, who values others and is valued by them for what he does and not for what he obtains....Only free people conscious of their worth and their equality can build a free society."[14]

On the practical level, Nyerere called for changes in the following key areas of the education system: school organisation; curriculum; and primary education structure. In the case of the school organisation structures, he argued that schools were to operate as communities in which pupils, teachers and others worked in a co-operative manner to maintain and develop their schools.

Accordingly he stated:

> Schools must, in fact, become communities—and communities which practise the precept of self-reliance. The teachers, workers, and pupils together must be the members of a social unit in the same way as parents, relatives, and children are the family unit. There must be the same kind of relationship between children and parents in the village. And the former community must realize, just as the latter do, that their life and well-being depend upon the production of wealth—by farming or other activities. This means that all schools, but especially secondary schools and other forms of higher education, must contribute to their own upkeep; they must be economic communities as well as social and educational communities.[15]

In Nyerere's view the creation of a socialist society required that school curriculum at all levels had to pay attention to the concrete realities of Tanzanian society. In this respect, there was to be more emphasis on agricultural development, the use of Swahili as a language of instruction and the learning of local and African cultural traditions and history. For Nyerere, the emphasis on agricultural education did not mean elimination of other aspects of education but was rather a reflection of his philosophy that the education system had to take local realities seriously and to serve the needs of the majority who were rural peasants. His call for an education that was relevant to local conditions was based on the clear understanding of the difficulties that Tanzania faced as a peripheral country with a predominantly agrarian rural economy. He nevertheless believed that despite these structural constraints the use of available resources "in a spirit of self-reliance" would provide real progress that affected "the lives of the masses, not just having spectacular show-pieces in the towns while the rest of the people of Tanzania live in their present poverty."[16]

In line with his view that education had to be geared to the needs of the majority and those of the country, Nyerere argued primary school education was to be reoriented in a manner that made it "a complete education in itself."[17] Under the inherited system, primary education was seen merely as a preparatory stage that paved the way for secondary school education for those who successfully passed the required examinations. For Nyerere, Tanzania's social and economic realities meant that only a few students made it to the secondary school, hence his calls for the need to restructure the primary school system education in order to better prepare the majority of the students for life in a rural agrarian-based economy.

As will be discussed latter, Nyerere's thinking on the role of education in Tanzania's development was a major contribution to development discourse. However, efforts to institute changes in the education system based on the ideas outlined in *Education for Self-Reliance* did not yield the results Nyerere had hoped for, leading him in 1974 to declare: "I am becoming increasingly convinced that we in Tanzania either have not yet found the right educational policy or have not yet succeeded in implementing it."[18] Examples from some areas targeted for major reforms show the contradictions that marked the implementations of goals advocated by Nyerere. Studies have shown some successes in schools such as Weruweru and Kibaha which established well-managed and productive farms among other projects.[19] In the majority of cases however, given the economic constraints of dependent capitalism there were no resources to establish and maintain viable economic activities.

Further, Nyerere's push to have students terminate their education after their primary education was resented by parents from the subordinate classes since children from the ruling class proceeded to institutions of higher learning without any constraints from the state. As Ishumi and Maliyamkono have stated, the targets of Nyerere's primary school policy "were the children of ordinary (peasant) parents rather than of all parents, including those highly placed in the Government bureaucracy and in the Party. In fact none of the children of the official category of parents went back to the village after the formal completion of, or after failing, the leaving examinations at primary or even secondary level."[20]

The contradiction that arose in the implementations of Nyerere's policy of primary education stemmed not only from his underestimation of the deepening of class divisions in the postcolonial era but also the limited shift in terms of ideological outlook among Tanzanians with regard to education. While Nyerere stressed that practical elements of education such as handicraft production and farming were as important as pure academic learning, for the majority of Tanzanians the colonial ideology that emphasised the latter remained. Commenting on this point in 1971 Lema stated:

> Still in the minds of most teachers, pupils, and parents, education is interpreted simply as academic book learning. The importance of practical education in skills such as handicrafts, and of social education in human relations, patterns of behaviour, and other attitudes of life is ignored....Everyone has come to regard academic studies as the most valuable prize in life — worth almost any sacrifice — while manual work is despised as an activity fit only for the illiterate and the 'school failures'.[21]

Nyerere and the power of Critical Education Theory

Notwithstanding the problems associated with the implementation of Nyerere's policy of education for self-reliance, his insights and those of other critical education theorists on the role of education in the evolution of socio-political and economic processes remain major contributions to social theory and practice. For Nyerere and other critical education theorists, education is viewed as a powerful instrument in the creation and reproduction of structures of domination. In his examination of the colonial education system, for instance, Nyerere showed the crucial role that this system played in facilitating the goals of the colonial regime. Elaborating on this issue, he claimed that the education system "was not designed to prepare young people for service of their country; instead it was motivated by a desire to inculcate the values of the colonial society and to train individuals for the service of the colonial state......It emphasized and encouraged the individualistic instincts of mankind, instead of his co-operative instincts. It led to the possession of individual material wealth being the major criterion of social merit and worth."[22]

Echoing Nyerere's view on the role of education systems in perpetuating the structures of domination Shor and Freire state:

> The curriculum is presented as normative, neutral and benevolent, even as it "cools you out," adjusting most students to subordinate positions in society. Inequality is presented as natural, just, and earned, given the differing "aptitudes" and "achievements" of various groups. The advantages of the elite are hidden behind a myth of "equal opportunity" while the idiom of the elites is named "correct usage," another myth of symbolic violence against colloquial speech, making the idioms of the ordinary people into inferior, outlaw languages. This social construction of inequality through schooling joins a constellation of other agencies repeating the messages and myths, in the mass media, mass advertisements, and the job market. For individual students, it becomes hard to see alternatives to the way things are and have to be.[23]

Arguing along similar lines, Connell has demonstrated how the ruling class uses schools to reproduce itself. In this regard he states:

> The school generates practices by which the [ruling] class is renewed, integrated, and re-constituted in the face of changes in its own composition and in the general social circumstances in which it tries to survive and prosper. (This is an embracing practice, ranging from the school fete, Saturday sport, and week-night dinners with parents, to the organization of a marriage market—e.g., interschool dances—and informal networks in business and the professions, to the regulation of class membership, updating ideology, and subordination of particular interests to those of class as a whole.) The ruling-class school is no mere agent of the class; it is an important and active part of it. In short, it is organic to its class. Bourdieu wrote a famous essay about the school as conserver; we would suggest an equal stress should be laid on the school as constructor.[24]

The education system has also historically been used to promote and reproduce the ideology of racial inferiority among non-white communities. For example, in the context of the history of education in the United States bell hooks contends that the education structure played a central role in the entrenchment of racist ideology. Using the Columbus narrative as an example hooks states:

> We were taught that the Indians would have conquered and dominated white folk explorers if they could have but they were simply not strong or smart enough. Embedded in all these teachings was the assumption that it was the whiteness of these explorers in the "New World" that gave them greater power. The word 'whiteness" was never used. The key word, the one that was synonymous with whiteness, was "civilization."[25]

Other critical education theorists have shown how the education system serves the needs of a society's economic model. On the link between the education system and American capitalism Bowles and Gintis state:

> The educational system helps integrate youth into the economic system, we believe, through a structural correspondence between its social relations and those of production. The structure of social relations in education not only inures the student to the discipline of the workplace, but develops the types of personal demeanor, modes of self-preservation, self-image, and social identifications which are crucial ingredients of job adequacy. Specifically, the social relationships of education—the relationships between administrators and teachers, teachers and students, students and their work—replicate the hierarchical division of labor.[26]

In addition to its role in the creation and maintenance of structures of domination, Nyerere saw education as an important tool in the struggle for liberation from all forms of oppression. According to Nyerere education under the *ujamaa* development framework was to encourage the emergence of liberated citizens "able to think for themselves, to make judgements on all the issues affecting them; they have to be able to interpret the decisions made through the democratic institutions of our society, and to implement them in the light of the peculiar local circumstances where they happen to live."[27] For Nyerere education was to liberate people not only on the economic and political front but also psychologically. Reminding teachers of their role in the struggle for psychological liberation he stated that: "You will teach to produce clerks as the colonialists did. You will not be teaching fighters but a bunch of slaves and semi-slaves. Get your pupils out of the colonial mentality. You have to produce tough people; stubborn youths—who can do something—not hopeless youths."[28]

Freire also saw education as playing a vital role in the struggle for liberation. In this respect he criticized mainstream education which he claimed was afflicted by a "narration sickness" driven by a "banking" approach to education in which:

> Education becomes an act of depositing in which the students are the depositories and the teacher is the depositor. Instead of communicating, the teacher issues communiques and makes deposits which the students patiently receive, memorize, and repeat....In the banking concept of education, knowledge is a gift bestowed by those who consider themselves knowledgeable upon those whom they consider to know nothing....The more students work at storing the deposits entrusted to them, the less they develop the critical consciousness which would result from their intervention in the world as transformers of that world.[29]

Consequently, Freire like Nyerere called for the re-orientation of traditional schooling systems. In his case Freire proposed the theory and practice of "problem-posing" education whose central goal was to aid students both young and old with "the emergence of consciousness and critical intervention in reality."[30] For Freire, this approach to education was pregnant with revolutionary potential:

> Those who, in learning to read and write, come to a new awareness of selfhood and begin to look critically at the social situation in which they find themselves, often take the initiative in acting to transform the society that has denied them this opportunity of participation. Education is once again a subversive force.[31]

While those working from traditional education theory viewed education as an instrument for *individual* liberation, Nyerere and Freire saw education as something that contributes to the transformation of the society as a whole. For Nyerere, to achieve this goal the education system was to:

> foster the social goals of living together, and working together, for the common good. It has to prepare our young people to play a dynamic and constructive part in the development of a society in which all members share fairly in the good or bad fortune of the group, and in which progress is measured in terms of human well-being, not prestige buildings, cars, or other

such things, whether privately or publicly owned. Our education must therefore inculcate a sense of commitment to the total community, and help the pupils to accept the values appropriate to our kind of future, not those appropriate to our colonial past.[32]

In Freire's case he stated that:

I don't believe in self-liberation. Liberation is a social act....Even when you individually feel yourself most free, if this feeling is not a social feeling, if you are not able to use your recent freedom to help others to be free by transforming the totality of society, then you are exercising only an individualist attitude towards empowerment or freedom.[33]

Thus for Nyerere and Freire liberation for the whole society could not be achieved by individual self-awakening — important as this was to the struggle. Rather it was to be attained by the coming together of social forces in specific historical settings to struggle for transformative change. This view of liberation as a historical act echoes the declaration by Marx and Engles that "Liberation" is a historical and not a mental act.[34]

To sum up, it is contended here that while Nyerere's critical education thought and that of others working from this perspective has its limitations, it nevertheless provides a powerful analytical tool in the exploration of the role of education in specific historical circumstances. In the context of development discourse and practice, this tradition shows that even within the boundaries set by local and international political and economic structures education can provide the necessary tools in the struggle for social change. In this respect critical education theory offers an important antidote to the embracing pessimism that generally permeates development discourse. Specifically, in an era dominated by market-driven politics under which schools are geared to the production of "credentialized workers for whom the demands of citizenship are subordinated to the vicissitudes of the market place and the commercial public sphere,"[35] Nyerere's and Freire's rich "language of possibility"[36] gives us hope for the future since it reminds us that history has not ended.

Endnotes

1 David R. Morrison, *Education and Politics in Africa: The Tanzania Case.* Montreal: McGill-Queen's University Press, 1976, pp. 51-52

2 Walter Rodney, "Education and Tanzania Socialism", in Idrian N. Resnick (ed.), *Tanzania: Revolution by Education.* Arusha: Longmans, 1968, p. 71.

3 Agrippah T. Mugomba, "African Mind Processing: Colonial Miseducation and Elite Psychological Decolonization", in Agrippah T. Mugomba and Mougo Nyaggah (eds.), *Independence without Freedom.* Oxford: Clico Press, 1980, p. 42.

4 Rodney, op. cit., p. 76.

5 For a full text of this booklet see Julius Nyerere, *Ujamaa — Essays on Socialism.* London: Oxford University Press, 1968.

6 Ibid., p. 47.

7 Ibid., p. 54.

8 Ibid., p. 55.

9 Ibid.

10 Ibid., p. 56.

11 Ibid., p. 55.

12 Ibid., p. 49.

13 Ibid., p. 52.

14 Ibid., pp. 53-54.

15 Ibid., p. 64.

16 Ibid., p. 51.

17 Ibid., p. 61.

18 Nyerere quoted in "Education for Liberation", in *Documents on Adult Education*, No. 1. Dar es Salaam: Institute of Adult Education, 1974.

19 Ishumi and Maliyamkono, op. cit., p. 53.

20 A.G. Ishumi & T.L. Maliyamkono, "Education for Self-Reliance", in Colin Legum and Geoffrey Mari (eds.), *Mwalimu: The Influence of Nyerere*, p. 54.

21 A.A. Lema, "Education for Self-Reliance: A Brief Survey of Self-Reliant Activities in some Tanzanian Schools and Colleges". Dar es Salaam: Institute of Education, University of Dar es Salaam, p. 27.

22 Ibid., p. 47.

23 Ira Shor and Paulo Freire, *A Pedagogy for Liberation: Dialogues on Transforming Education*. South Hadley, MA: Bergin & Garvey, 1987, p. 123.

24 R.W. Connell, *et al.*, "Class and Gender Dynamics in a Ruling-Class School", *Interchange* 12, 1981.

25 bell hooks, *Outlaw culture: Resisting representations*. New York: Routledge, 1994b, p. 199.

26 S. Bowels and H. Gintis, *Schooling in Capitalist America*. New York: Basic Books, 1976.

27 Ibid., p. 53.

28 Cited in Ngugi wa Thiong'o, *Moving the Centre: The Struggle for Cultural Freedoms*. London: James Currey, 1993, p. 166

29 Paulo Freire, *Pedagogy of the Oppressed*. New York: Continuum, 1970, pp. 58 and 60.

30 Ibid.

31 Ibid.

32 Ibid., p. 52.

33 Shor and Freire, op. cit., p. 109.

34 K. Marx and F. Engels, *The German Ideology.* Moscow: Progress Publishers, 1976, p. 44.

35 Henry A. Giroux, *Series Foreword*, in Florence Namulundah, *bell hooks' Engaged Pedagogy: A Transgressive Education for Critical Consciousness.* Westport: Bergin & Garvey, 1998, p. ix.

36 Henry A. Giroux, quoted in "Editors' Introduction: Absent discourses: Paulo Freire and the dangerous memories of liberation", in Peter McLaren and Peter Leonard (eds.), *Paulo Freire: A critical encounter.* London: Routledge, 1993, p. 3.

CHAPTER EIGHT

Inspiration for a New Generation?

COMPARING NYERERE, MANDELA AND MBEKI

David A. McDonald

People can say [our policy] is Thatcherite, but for this country, privatisation is the fundamental policy of our government. Nelson Mandela[1]

Call me a Thatcherite. Thabo Mbeki[2]

In Chapter Six of this volume, Colin Leys makes the observation "that it was something special to be young [during the early years of Nyerere's political leadership in Tanzania], and to be in a country with such an inspiring, young leader." Virtually every left-leaning academic and activist of Leys' generation seems to agree. Thirty years later, however, the center of political gravity on the continent has shifted to South Africa, where the question of inspirational leadership is far more controversial.

This chapter lays out, in the spirit of this collection, my own thoughts as a young researcher in post-apartheid South Africa and a comparison of the leadership styles and principles of Nelson Mandela and his successor Thabo Mbeki with those of Nyerere in Tanzania. The contexts, of course, are very different and it is impossible to make direct comparisons, but the essence of the leadership in these two countries, it seems to me, are as different as night and day, with Mbeki in particular doing as much to alienate the left in South Africa as Nyerere did to embrace it in Tanzania.

This was not always the case. In the early 1990s there was much to be inspired by in South Africa when it came to political leadership. Nelson Mandela, after 27 years of imprisonment, much of it in isolation and hard labour, emerged from his prison cell to forgive his captors and to call for peace and reconciliation. Although thousands were to die in political clashes leading up to the first democratic elections in 1994, millions of South Africans were deeply moved by the depth of his generosity of spirit and many more thousands of lives were undoubtedly spared as a result of his moral vision (and accompanying moral authority).

So too is Mandela to be commended for his announcement, before he was elected President in 1994, that he would stay in office for only one term. As others have noted in this volume about Nyerere in his time, Mandela's democratic departure from office has made an important continental statement about the need for transparent and constitutionally sound transitions of leadership (in direct contrast to the authoritarianism of many leaders in the region such as Robert Mugabe of Zimbabwe).

Most importantly, there was much inspiration to be found in the policymaking circles of Mandela and Mbeki in the early to mid-1990s. From the highly redistributional principles of the early drafts of the Reconstruction and Development Programme (RDP) to the land reform promises, primary health care changes and plans to revise educational spending and curricula, South Africa offered some of the most progressive and even socialist policy reforms in the world at the time. The introduction of the transitional Constitution in 1993 (finalized in 1996) also had the effect of formalizing many of the basic human rights advocated by the ANC's socialist wings: guaranteed access to basic services by all; the right to a healthy and safe environment; race and gender equity; and so on.

South Africa became a magnet for left-leaning scholars and activists from throughout the continent and beyond in the early 1990s, and there was an enormous blossoming of political discourse and debate within South Africa's own progressive movements. With the end of apartheid came also the end of dogmatic political orthodoxies and an explosion of environmental, feminist, poststructuralist and neo-Marxist debates. South Africa was arguably the most politically and intellectually exciting place to be in Africa — if not in the entire world — at that time. Not all of this excitement was due to leadership from the top — social justice struggles go very deep in South Africa — but the progressive orientation of leaders like Mandela and Mbeki played no small part in creating this political dynamism.

Ultimately, however, there was to be much disappointment on the left, particularly with respect to economic policy. After decades of speeches and policy papers about nationalization and some form of nascent socialism after apartheid — not to mention the more concrete promises of access to basic services like water and sanitation and a redistribution of land in the African National Congress' (ANC) pre-election manifesto, the Reconstruction and Development Programme — the ANC moved relatively quickly after it was elected to office in 1994 to introduce far-reaching neoliberal policy positions on a wide range of economic questions (e.g., trade liberalization, fiscal and monetary policy, privatization).

ANC economic policy of today has moved a long way from the anti-capitalist spirit of the party's famous Freedom Charter of 1955, captured here under the heading "The People Shall Share in the Country's Wealth!":

> The national wealth of our country, the heritage of South Africans, shall be restored to the people; The mineral wealth beneath the soil, the Banks and monopoly industry shall be transferred to the ownership of the people as a whole; All other industry and trade shall be controlled to assist the well-being of the people; All people shall have equal rights to trade where they choose, to manufacture and to enter all trades, crafts and professions.

One cannot help but feel that there was a loss of political will at the leadership level which has precipitated much of this slide — political will of the sort that Nyerere apparently had much of in the 1960s and early 1970s. Neither Mandela nor Mbeki has demonstrated that kind of commitment to socialist principles, despite their party's long rhetorical association with socialism.

At one level, we should not be surprised. Neither Mandela nor Mbeki ever claimed to be socialists themselves. In fact, both have long claimed just the opposite.[3]

Nevertheless, the degree to which they have distanced themselves from even the mildest of socialist demands is quite remarkable, as is the pace at which neoliberal reforms have been introduced. Even George Soros, international financier and Mbeki confidante, has remarked that, "Today South Africa is very much in the hands of international capital."[4]

Far from being an inspiration to those on the left, South African political leadership has become something of an ideological Goliath — a power that intimidates those who challenge its authority while at the same time minimizing the space for critical debate. In many ways South Africa has become an uncomfortable place to be for those on the left and there can be no doubt that some of this ideological pressure is coming from the top.

There is also a considerable amount of 'talk left, act right' behaviour amongst ANC leadership making it difficult at times to challenge and assess the policy agenda of the government. Mbeki is most notable in this respect, employing socialist rhetoric when the occasion calls for it (labour union meetings, community rallies, etc.), but just as quickly switching to the language of corporate board rooms and fiscal restraint when it comes to actual policy decisions.

Mandela, too, has had many rhetorical flip-flops, perhaps the most famous of which was his announcement on the day he was released from prison in 1990 that nationalization was still a key policy of the ANC, only to be retracted shortly thereafter when pressured by the banks and mining conglomerates. As the *Business Day* noted in 1993: "We can look with some hope to the evolution in economic thinking in the ANC since the occasion nearly three years ago when Nelson Mandela stepped out of prison and promptly reaffirmed his belief in the nationalisation of the heights of the economy. By contrast...Mandela [has gone] out of his way to assure a large group of foreign (and local) journalists that the ANC was now as business-friendly as any potential foreign investor could reasonably ask. He indicated further that ANC economic thinking was now being influenced as much by Finance Minister Derek Keys and by organised business as anyone else." And in Mandela's own words: "[The ANC is] determined to...establish the political and social climate which is necessary to ensure business confidence and create the possibility for all investors to make long-term commitments."[5]

There Is No Alternative?

But perhaps these criticisms are too harsh. As critical as one may be of this ideological shift in leadership, it must nevertheless be understood in the context of a dramatic swing to the right in global political discourse in the post–Cold War era. With the collapse of the Soviet Union , a long-time ANC benefactor, the stage was set for the rapid spread of neoliberal policymaking in South Africa under the auspices of the World Bank and other multilateral and bilateral donor agencies. Some of this policy pressure was admirably resisted by the ANC in the lead-up to the 1994 election (the refusal to negotiate large, hard-currency loans from the World Bank being the most notable), but as dozens of commentators have noted since 1994, the ANC has accepted neoliberal orthodoxy in virtually every other sphere of policy — from housing to land reform to health care and urban infrastructure.[6]

One could argue here that Tanzania in the 1960s and 1970s was under similar levels of pressure from the right and yet it managed to stay the socialist course for quite a bit longer. In Nyerere's time this right-wing triumphalism manifested itself in different, and in some ways more openly violent, ways as a result of the Cold War. But Tanzania at that time had a counter-hegemonic fall-back option in the form of Soviet and/or Chinese assistance, along with the moral support of a host of other 'third world' socialist (or socialist-leaning) allies on the continent and elsewhere. South Africa, on the other hand, gained its independence in an era of unprecedented hegemonic authority: a time when socialism was considered 'dead' and even mild Keynesianism was deemed foolish. Capital can now be moved around the globe in seconds at the push of a button and similarly speedy forms of capital flight or currency speculation can mean ruin for a country overnight (as George Soros knows well). As squeezed as Tanzania was vis-à-vis global capitalism in the 1960s and 1970s, South Africa in the 1990s found itself with even less room, and less time, for political and economic maneuver.

But it must also be kept in mind that South Africa's economy is more than 16 times larger than that of Tanzania in absolute terms and more than 13 times larger in per capita terms.[7] It is also much more industrialized and diversified than Tanzania's economy ever was (despite the relative narrowness of the South African economic base in global terms[8]) with internationally competitive mining firms and reasonably strong domestic consumer and agricultural industries. This economic base, combined with a highly politicized and organized labour and civic movement broadly allied to the South African Communist Party, made South Africa a much more likely candidate than Tanzania in both material and ideological terms for a successful post-independence run at socialism.

Why then did South Africa give up on a socialist alternative so quickly? Was it a question of leadership? John Saul, another contributor to this volume, has commented on this question elsewhere as follows: "Some will perhaps find it difficult not to be sympathetic to the current leaders of the ANC, given the pressures they've been under. Nonetheless, it's equally difficult to escape the feeling — historians will decide — that in some important way these leaders have merely blown it."[9]

There Must Be an Alternative

Blown it? In many ways we will never know what the immediate post-apartheid alternatives might have been. Proponents of the neoliberal path argue that any attempts at nationalization or radical redistribution of property/wealth would have resulted in massive capital and human flight from the country as well as possible civil war and/or sabotage of socialist policies.

What we do know is that many of the ANC's ambitious plans for reconstruction and development have begun to crumble under the weight of an unforgiving policy of fiscal restraint and trickle-down economics. There has been no significant movement on the issue of land reform, for example, and millions are still without homes and basic services. To make matters worse, for many of those that have received new services since 1994 the neoliberal principals of cost recovery and cut-offs for non-payment have meant that hundreds of thousands of rural and urban poor are without these amenities once again.[10]

Discontent with neoliberal policies is growing in South Africa. In mid-2001 over four million workers went on strike for two days to oppose the privatization of public services such as railways, telecommunications and water. Township activists now *toi-toi* in front of the homes and offices of their erstwhile comrades and there are growing and well-orchestrated campaigns to re-connect poor households to services like water and electricity when the state (or a private sector service provider) cuts them off for non-payment.

The maxim frequently heard on the left today in South Africa is that There Must Be an Alternative (THEMBA) to neoliberalism — a deliberate and ironic twist on Thatcher's famous TINA (There Is No Alternative) acronym. That neither Mandela nor Mbeki has lent support for this search for alternatives — Mbeki has in fact gone out of his way to belittle and demonize vocal opponents on the left — suggests that they have indeed "blown it" as far as the creation of intellectual space for a workable form of socialism in South and Southern Africa is concerned.

Conclusion

The ideological shift that has taken place in South Africa since the early 1990s cannot be overstated. As John Saul also noted after a term teaching sociology at the University of the Witwatersrand shortly after this conference on Nyerere was held, "My strongest impression of the new South Africa is just how easy, in many circles, it has become to be considered an 'ultra- leftist."[11]

Granted, this is a far cry from the nasty days of apartheid thuggery where dissent could mean forced exile, a lengthy prison term, or even death. In this respect South Africa is a true liberal democracy, with all its apparent freedoms, and is a safe place to be for an academic. But socialist it is not, and for those on the left there is increasingly less to feel inspired about from political leadership in the country.

In the end, the real inspiration on the left in South Africa today comes from the growing cadre of unionists, civic organizers and political leaders on the ground who share a commitment to the principles of economic equity, social justice and socialist policy. It is here that the ghost of Nyerere is perhaps the strongest in South Africa, with a leadership creed scattered, as Nyerere would no doubt have wanted it to be, amongst those closest to the daily grind of poverty.

Endnotes

1 As quoted in J. Pilger, *Hidden Agendas*. London: Vintage, 1998, p. 606.

2 As quoted in *Business Times* (Johannesburg), 16 June 1996.

3 Mandela: "In our economic policies... there is not a single reference to things like nationalisation, and this is not accidental. There is not a single slogan that will connect us with any Marxist ideology" (as quoted in Hein Marais, *South Africa: Limits to Change*. London: Zed Books, 1998, p.146; Mbeki: "The ANC is not a socialist party. It has never pretended to be one, it has never said it was, and it is not trying to be. It will not become one by decree or for the purpose of pleasing its 'left' critics" (taken from a 1984 article in *the Canadian Journal of African Studies*, as quoted in the *Mail & Guardian*, 23 June 2000).

4 Taken from the film by B. Cashdan (2001), *Globalisation: Whose Side are We On?*, Johannesburg, recorded in January, 2001, Davos.

5 *Business Day*, 13 January 1993; *Financial Mail*, 7 February 1992. These additional quotes by Mandela provide further indication of just how far Mandela was to move on this issue: "Nationalisation is like the sword of Damocles hanging over those who want to invest. So long as nationalisation is our policy, we will not attract investors" (*Financial Times*, November 1991); [Returning from a conference in Davos, Switzerland]: "They changed my views altogether. I came home to say: 'Chaps, we have to choose. We either keep nationalisation and get no investment, or we modify our own attitude and get investment" (quoted in A. Sampson, *Nelson Mandela: The Authorised Biography*. Johannesburg: Jonathan Ball, 1999, 435. I am indebted to Ian Taylor and Simon Kimani Ndung'u for several of these references.

6 See for example, Hein Marais, *South Africa: Limits to Change: The Political Economy of Transition*. London: Zed Press, 2001; Patrick Bond, *Elite Transition: From Apartheid to Neoliberalism in South Africa*. London: Pluto Press, 1999.

7 Figures are for mainland Tanzania only. Data taken from World Bank, *World Development Report: Attacking Poverty 2000/2001*. New York: Oxford University Press, 2001, p. 275.

8 On this point see Ben Fine and Zavereh Rustonjee, *The Political Economy of South Africa: From Minerals-Energy Complex to Industrialisation*. London: Hurst and Company, 1996.

9 John Saul, "SA's Tragic Leap to the Right", *Mail & Guardian*, 23 June 2000.

10 See for example, Patrick Bond and Meshack Khosa (eds.), *An RDP Policy Audit*. HSRC: Pretoria, 2000; Maj Fiil-Flynn, *The Electricity Crisis in Soweto*, Occasional Paper No. 4. Cape Town: Municipal Services Project, 2001.

11 John Saul, "SA's Tragic Leap to the Right", *Mail & Guardian*, 23 June 2000.

Appendix

Defining Socialism in Tanzania

Julius K. Nyerere

This appendix is a reproduction of the Introduction to Nyerere's 1968 book Uhuru na Ujamaa: Freedom and Socialism (by kind permission of the publishers, Oxford University Press (Tanzania). The paper is a description of Nyerere's vision of socialism and is intended, in his own words, to "enlarge upon the socialist goal which Tanzania has accepted as its objective, and upon the manner in which Tanzania can progress towards this goal." The paper is reproduced here for several reasons. First, it demonstrates the incredibly articulate and alive manner in which Nyerere spoke and wrote and is an eloquent example of his formidable writing style. Second, the paper provides an intellectually rigorous description of what socialism means in an African context. It is non-dogmatic in its allowance for different versions of social, political and economic life under the banner of 'socialism' while at the same time insisting on a core set of values and material realities. In this sense, the paper is still very contemporary. But perhaps most important of all is that the paper reminds us, in this era of neoliberal hegemony, that a more just and equitable word is possible. Whether or not we still use the term 'socialism', Nyerere's description of the possibilities (and the challenges) of a post-capitalist world are as exciting today as they were over 30 years ago.

* * * *

The Tanganyika African National Union has been formally committed to socialism since it revised its constitution almost immediately after Tanganyika's independence in December 1961. Much of the legislation and many of the policies adopted by the different Governments—both before and after the Union with Zanzibar—reflected that commitment. Yet it gradually became clear that the absence of a generally accepted and easily understood statement of philosophy and policy was causing problems, and some Government and Party actions were having the effect of encouraging the growth of non-socialist institutions, values, and attitudes. This was happening because the implications of our broad commitment to socialism were not understood. The adoption of the Arusha Declaration early in 1967 therefore marks an important step forward for Tanzania. For this Declaration, together with subsequent policy statements, provides some definition of what socialism demands of our country, and especially of its leaders.

But the Arusha Declaration is only a beginning. Tanzania is not now a socialist country; it is only a country whose people have firmly committed themselves to building socialism. The actual work has barely begun. For socialism is not built by Government decisions, nor by Acts of Parliament; a country does not become socialist by nationalizations or grand designs on paper. It is more difficult than that to build socialism, and it takes much longer.

Ujamaa Iis Tanzanian Socialism

What does socialism mean for us? How can we move towards it? The answer to these questions is in some ways implicit in the word we have chosen to describe our goal. For there was nothing accidental in our selection of the word 'ujamaa' to define our socialist policies; nor did this word result solely from the desire to find a Swahili equivalent for the word 'socialism'. Swahili is a growing language and continues to incorporate foreign words into its vocabulary when necessary; indeed we talk of the policies of some other countries as being 'kisoshalisti'. The word 'ujamaa' was chosen for special reasons. First, it is an African word and thus emphasizes the African-ness of the policies we intend to follow. Second, its literal meaning is 'family-hood', so that it brings to the mind of our people the idea of mutual involvement in the family as we know it.

By the use of the word 'ujamaa', therefore, we state that for us socialism involves building on the foundation of our past, and building also to our own design. We are not importing a foreign ideology into Tanzania and trying to smother our distinct social patterns with it. We have deliberately decided to grow, as a society, out of our own roots, but in a particular direction and towards a particular kind of objective. We are doing this by emphasizing certain characteristics of our traditional organization, and extending them so that they can embrace the possibilities of modern technology and enable us to meet the challenge of life in the twentieth century world.

This emphasis on growth from traditional patterns of social living means that we shall be trying to create something which is uniquely ours, and by methods which may be unique to Tanzania. This does not invalidate our claim to be building socialism.

Socialism is international; its ideas and beliefs relate to man in society, not just to Tanzanian man in Tanzania, or African man in Africa. But just because it is a universal concept so it must also relate to Tanzanian man in Tanzania. And if it is to do this, it must be able to encompass us as we are—as our geography and our history have made us. It must not demand the remoulding of man to a single pattern, regardless of whether man has been born in Uzanaki or Hunan, Colchester or Uppsala. The universality of socialism only exists if it can take account of men's differences, and be equally valid for all of them. And it can. For the universality of socialism does not imply a single, world-wide uniformity of social institutions, social habits, or social language. There is no reason why a dozen fully socialist societies should not have a dozen different methods of organizing themselves, a dozen different sets of customs relating to social intercourse, and a dozen different styles of political address and description. It is by no means necessary to call people 'comrade' in order to be socialist; it is not necessary to insist upon a civil marriage ceremony in a socialist society; it is by no means certain that a centralized economy is an inherent part of socialist organization. It is my contention that socialist societies in different parts of the world will differ in many respects even when they are fully developed instead of

being, as now, at different stages on the road to socialism. The differences between these societies will reflect both the manner of their development, and
their historical traditions.

It would be absurd to suggest that because differences will exist between different socialist societies in different parts of the world, that therefore 'socialism' has
no meaning, or that it is too vague a concept to be sensibly adopted as the social
goal of a young country. For there are certain universal values and essential
characteristics which would be found in every socialist society, and which would
not be found in non-socialist societies. It is the existence of these values and
characteristics which define a socialist society. They will not necessarily be found
in a society which is still creating socialism; a society in transition is, by definition, short of the goal. But the more of these values and characteristics which
can be observed in the workings of any community the nearer it is to becoming
socialist. The gap between the reality and the goal will show the distance which
has still to be travelled and the work which still has to be done. A brief examination of these essential elements of socialism will demonstrate to those who know
Tanzania the amount of hard work which our country still has to perform.

What is a Socialist Society?

What should we look for when trying to determine whether a particular society
is socialist? What are the universal characteristics and values which would un-
derlie differences of institution and organization in a socialist society?

First, and most central of all, is that under socialism Man is the purpose of all
social activity. The service of man, the furtherance of his human development, is
in fact the purpose of society itself. There is no other purpose above this; no
glorification of 'nation', no increase in production—nothing is more central to a
socialist society than an acceptance that Man is its justification for existence.

In one sense, all the other characteristics of socialism follow from this. But in
view of the historical development of mankind, one more thing has to be stated
categorically. The word 'man' to a socialist, means all men—all human beings.
Male and female; black, white, brown, yellow; long-nosed and short-nosed; educated and uneducated; wise and stupid; strong and weak; all these, and all other
distinctions between human beings, are irrelevant to the fact that all members of
the society—all the human beings who are its purpose—are equal.

The equality of man may or may not be susceptible to scientific proof. But its acceptance as a basic assumption of life in society is the core and essence of socialism. No one who qualifies his belief in the equality of man is really a socialist. A society is not socialist if, in its organization, or its practices, it discriminates, or allows discrimination, between its members because of their parentage, their place of birth, their appearance, their religious beliefs, or any thing other than their behaviour in relation to their fellows. The existence of racialism, of tribalism, or of religious intolerance, means that a society is not socialist—regardless of whatever other attributes it may have. A society in which all men are of equal account will probably be socialist, because socialist organization is really the means by which the diversity of mankind is harnessed to the common benefit of all men. Socialism, as a system, is in fact the organization of men's inequalities to serve their equality. Their equality is socialist belief.

The upholding of human dignity could be expected to follow automatically from these two basic characteristics of a socialist society. For a society cannot acquiesce in the abasement or humiliation of its own purpose; on the contrary, a man-centred society would promote the dignity and the growth to excellence of all the human beings who are members of it. Indeed, it could not draw boundaries around itself in this matter. A socialist society would seek to uphold human dignity everywhere; and however limited its capacity in this respect, it could never act in such a manner as to be itself responsible for the denial of any man's humanity.

Democracy is another essential characteristic of a socialist society. For the people's equality must be reflected in the political organization; everyone must be an equal participant in the government of his society. Whatever devices are used to implement this principle, the people (meaning all the members of the society equally) must be sovereign, and they must be able to exert their sovereignty without causing a break-down of the law and order, or of the administration in their society. There must, in other words, be some mechanisms by which the people exert their will peacefully, and achieve changes in the laws which govern them; they must be able to change the personnel in positions of leadership within the framework of the normal workings of the social system. It is difficult to see how this could be achieved without the existence of some system of free elections if the society is so large that direct democracy (the direct government by all the people) is impossible. But elections are not the beginning and end of democracy. The freedom of the people to choose their own representatives is important, but it is equally important that the people's representatives should possess the freedom and the power to exert effective control over those sectors of the social organization for which they have been given responsibility. And none of these things is possible unless every other aspect of society—its economic, social and legal organization— is such as to emphasize and serve man's equality. A political democracy which exists in a society of gross economic inequalities, or of social inequality, is at best imperfect, and at worst a hollow sham.

A socialist society, therefore, will consist of workers—and only of workers. Every member will contribute, by his work, to the total of wealth and welfare produced by the society, and he will receive a return in proportion to his efforts and his contribution to the wellbeing of the community. Only small children, the men and women who are too old to work, and the sick, are exempt from the responsibility to work. To everyone else this duty, and this right, belongs.

For work is not only a duty to society; it is also a right of every human being, and anyone who is deprived of the opportunity to do something useful for himself, his fellow citizens, and his society, needs and merits some compensation. The child needs food, love, and care; that is obvious and unquestioned. The sick and crippled need an opportunity to do whatever is within their power, and also the willing gift of such food, clothing and shelter as they are unable to provide for themselves. And the society has a responsibility also towards any person whom it deprives of an opportunity to earn his own living. Under socialism there could not be a group of 'permanently unemployed'; but technological changes, and the economic flexibility which must exist in a developing community, may mean that some individuals need support while they are receiving new training, or—especially in a country like Tanzania— until the first harvest when they return to the land.

Apart from these groups, however, everyone in a socialist society will be a worker. Unless this is so socialism cannot exist; it would collapse through its own poverty. But the word 'worker' in this context means anyone who works; he may be a peasant working on his own shamba, a member of a co-operative farming group, or a woman looking after her small children and the family home. None of these people receive wages for their activity, but they do contribute to the total output of goods and welfare. Nor is it necessary to make a distinction between a wage-earner whose work involves much physical labour, and one who works in an office or carries managerial or professional responsibilities. All who contribute to the society by their work are workers.

It follows from this that in a socialist society there will be no exploitation of one man by another. There will be no 'masters' who sit in idleness while others labour on 'their' farms or in 'their' factories. Nor will there be too great a degree of inequality between the incomes of different members of the society. It is arguable that an especially clever man, or an especially hard-working man, contributes more to the society than one who does not have these qualities, and that he is therefore entitled to receive greater remuneration. But can any one man do work which is 100 times more valuable than that of another? It is true that for some jobs to be done effectively certain extra facilities are needed by the worker; a teacher or an administrator, for example, will need a place where he can study quietly, will need to be able to obtain books of a certain type, and so on. But does anyone need a palace while another receives only a 'bedspace'?

There is, however, another form of exploitation which a socialist society would avoid, and to which it may be especially prone. A man who cheats his fellows by dishonesty, who fails to do a full day's work, or who fails to co-operate with his fellows because he wants to bolster his own personal interests, is exploiting other men. Society has as much a right, and a duty, to prevent these kinds of exploitation as it has to prevent the exploitation which arises from individual ownership of the means of production and exchange.

For this is another characteristic of a socialist community. It would be so organized that the tools of production and the mechanisms of exchange are firmly under the control of the people. Control in this context does not only mean regulation in the negative sense of stopping people from doing certain things. It also means the power to do positive things—to expand a factory, to build a new one in a particular place, to invest in a risky enterprise, etc. It seems almost certain that this will normally involve public ownership at least of the key points of the economy, and one would therefore expect a socialist society to be distinguished from a non-socialist society in this matter of ownership of the economy. It may be, however, that particular societies can devise some other means of securing effective and positive control over their economy in such a manner as to preclude exploitation. This would be unusual, but if they can, that society could still be recognized as socialist, provided that the other essential characteristics of socialism exist.

It may be necessary to add that public ownership can be of many types, and it has a purpose. The purpose is to ensure that there is no exploitation in the economy, and no built-in tendency towards inequalities. It could therefore be ownership by the people through the instrument of their elected central government, or their local government; or it could be expressed through co-operatives, or other group organizations. The appropriate form would vary both according to the technology concerned, and according to the other practices and desires of the society. The essential point is that no individual or group of individuals would be able to hold to ransom either the society as a whole, or other individuals, by means of their exclusive control of an instrument which is necessary to the increasing well-being of the community.

Obviously this does not preclude private ownership of the things which pertain to the individual worker, or to the family. Such a suggestion is simply put forward to frighten the timid men and to mislead those trying to find an alternative to the social evils of capitalism. A farmer can own his hoe, a carpenter can own his hand-saw; any worker can own the tools which he uses by himself as a supplement to his own hands. Similarly, a family can own the house in which it lives, the furniture and equipment which increase the comfort of its members, and so on. The question of public ownership arises when men have to co-operate together in the pursuit of a particular objective. When the tool has to be used by two men it must be owned equally; when the product is necessary for the decent life of others they must be involved in the control over it. Any suggestion that socialism involves the nationalization or community ownership of every artifact of life is the suggestion of a fool or a mischief-maker.

There is another bogeyman which is used to frighten people, and that is the suggestion that individual freedom does not exist under socialism. The purpose of socialism is to enlarge the real freedom of man, to expand his opportunity of living in dignity and well-being. An obviously essential part of this is that the laws of the society shall be known, be applied equally, and that people shall not be subject to arbitrary arrest, or persecution by the servants of the society. The Rule of Law is a part of socialism; until it prevails socialism does not prevail. By itself the Rule of Law does not bring socialism; but you cannot have socialism without it, because it is the expression of man's equality in one facet of social living.

The final characteristic of a socialist society which must be listed here is the social values it emphasizes. In a feudal or aristocratic system, birth is a matter of the highest importance; if you are born of certain parents you have social respect as well as economic advantages accorded to you as of right. In a capitalist system, individual wealth is the most important single criterion for respect, and the competitive spirit is acclaimed as a paramount social virtue—in practice if not in theory. The social values of a socialist society will be very different from either of these. First, both the organization and the teaching will emphasize man's co-operative spirit—his desire to work in harmony with his friends and neighbours—not his personal aggressiveness. Second, it will reserve its highest respect and its highest prizes for those whose life and work demonstrate the greatest service, not the greatest personal acquisitiveness. Comparative wealth will not be the criteria on which a man is judged by his fellows. Success in a socialist society will imply that a man has earned the respect, admiration, and love of his fellow citizens, by his desire to serve, and by the contribution he has made to the well-being of the community.

All these things together are the hallmark of a socialist society. When you find them you have found a society which is socialist. When you find some but not others, you have found a society which is partly socialist—or which has the elements of socialism in it. And when you find a deliberate attempt being made to build these values and organizational systems, then you have found a society which is working towards socialism.

Socialism and the Production of Wealth

Both before and since the Arusha Declaration, the Government and Party in Tanzania have been emphasizing the need to increase output—to increase the production of wealth. We shall continue to do this, because *in our circumstances* an increase in the amount of goods produced and available for social services, for distribution, and for investment, is a socialist purpose. Our country is bedevilled by its present poverty; people are sick, ignorant, and live in very poor conditions, because we do not produce enough wealth to be able to eradicate these evils. We have to increase our production of goods if we are to enable everyone to live in conditions of human dignity. At present not even complete equality in the distribution of the available wealth would do this; our national income per head is something between Shs. 400/- and Shs. 460/- per year. An increase in production must have a very high priority in our social plans; it is the cornerstone for all our other ambitions.

It is necessary to stress this because the production of wealth for its own sake is not a socialist purpose. The purpose of production must always be the greater well-being of man; goods must be produced because they are useful and make life better. To Tanzanians that looks very obvious; indeed, most Tanzanian citizens may wonder what I am talking about, because it is so obvious that extra food, bricks, roofing, ovens, chairs, tables, beds, clothing, and so on and so on, will make life better. Yet we are still in danger of being attracted by the idea of 'wealth' as represented by all the consumer goods we see advertised in foreign magazines (and even Tanzanian ones), or in the films, etc. We are still in danger of accepting the idea that the greatest production of consumer goods is the criterion by which a nation, or an economic system, should be judged.

A socialist does not look at things that way. He asks, what sort of production? What is it that is being produced? Under what conditions? And what effect does it have, on balance, on the society as a whole? To a socialist, therefore, there is no virtue in 'creating a market' for something which people have never thought of wanting and really have no need for, but which someone hopes to make a profit by producing. This happens all the time in capitalist societies; it is an inherent part of them. There are very many examples which could be given; I will mention only two. In some societies it is a matter of pride, I am told, to buy an electric tooth-brush—presumably the energy required to clean one's mouth properly is beyond the strength of well-fed men and women! An even more useless object which manufacturers were trying to persuade the people of another capitalist country to buy was something called a 'non-spill' tray, which was said to enable you to swing a tray holding glasses of liquid without spilling a drop! Advertisements to promote the sale of such things are a normal part of capitalist society; their newspapers, television, etc. make every attempt to suggest to people that they will be 'old-fashioned' if they do not acquire the object in question. In other words, an attempt is made to make people discontented without the thing which is being 'promoted', so that they will buy it—if they have enough money. This is called 'creating a market', and 'creating a market' is said to be an inherent part of progress', of increasing the national income, and of 'free consumer choice'.

A socialist will not be impressed by such values, nor even by the talk of people 'exercising their freedom as consumers', if, at the same time as these things are being produced and sold, other human values are being ignored or sacrificed. For the incredible thing is that in the same countries which encourage this kind of 'market creation', other people are living in conditions of great poverty, educational facilities are starved of funds, and completely free hospital care for everyone is said to be too expensive for the community to bear! The production of wealth for the benefit of man—that is production for socialist purposes—would have rather different results. Electric tooth-brushes and non-spill trays—if they were produced at all—would not be produced until after these more basic needs had been met.

To a socialist, the first priority of production must be the manufacture and distribution of such goods as will allow every member of the society to have sufficient food, clothing and shelter, to sustain a decent life. Other goods would be produced only if they in some way hastened the day when this goal was reached. Apart from these basic needs of man, a socialist society would put much emphasis on the production of socially advantageous goods. It would concentrate on better educational facilities, medical care, places of community activity like libraries, community centres, parks, etc. It would devote resources also to social values which have nothing to do with production—things like improving the hours and conditions of work, or maintaining and improving the natural beauties of the world in which we live. Of course, some care, money, and energy has to be spent on these non-consumer products even before the basic job is complete, because they affect the way people will be able to live. Thus, for example, when building new houses in a town it is necessary to plan for public spaces and leave room for community buildings even if you cannot build them immediately; it is necessary to provide minimum educational and health services as far as you can; and it is essential to spend that minimum amount of money which is necessary to prevent the destruction of that natural beauty or wild life which could never be replaced if it was once allowed to disappear.

In a socialist society, therefore, man as a consumer is not 'king'. Instead man is recognized as a human being who desires human dignity, who is a consumer both privately and socially, and who is also a producer. For socialism involves an acceptance of the fact that man's life in society cannot be divided up into bits. A man is concerned with his life as a whole; if he is starving it is no use expecting him to be happy because he has the freedom to vote every few years, or if he is well-fed it is no use expecting him to be happy as a slave. Under a socialist society men come together to try and organize the community in which they live so that all their different needs and all their co-operative social values are considered, with priority being given to those which are most urgent—but without any being destroyed.

In Tanzania the increased output of wealth so that all our people may live decently is the most urgent thing. But we cannot allow this need to destroy our belief in human equality and human dignity. On the contrary, we have to organize our expansion of wealth in such a way as to give the maximum possible emphasis to these other values.

Socialism is Secular

The fact that socialism is concerned with all aspects of man's life in society does not mean that man as an individual ceases to exist. Every person is unique; there are some things which are, and which must be, private to himself. Society has the right where necessary to regulate, encourage, or discourage, those actions of individuals which affect other members of the society. It has no business in relation to things which are by nature or by method entirely personal. Once a man has fulfilled his responsibilities to the society, it is nothing to do with socialism whether he spends his spare time painting, dancing, writing poetry, playing football, or just sitting. Nor is it any business of socialism if an individual is, or is not, inspired in his daily life by a belief in God, nor if he does, or does not, attend a place of religious worship—or pray elsewhere.

Socialism is concerned with man's life in *this* society. A man's relationship with his God is a personal matter for him and him alone; his beliefs about the hereafter are his own affair. These things have nothing to do with anyone else as long as he does not indulge in practices which adversely affect the similar private rights of other members of the society. Thus, for example, a man's belief that he should pray at specified hours of the day and night wherever he happens to be is a matter for him, and no one else has the right to interfere. But a religion which involved human sacrifice, or demanded the exploitation of human beings, could not be allowed to carry out these practices.

Socialism's concern about the organization of life on earth does not involve any supposition about life elsewhere, or about man's soul, or the procedures for fulfilling the will of God or Gods. Socialism is secular. It has nothing to say about whether there is a God. Certainly it rests on the assumption of the equality of man, but people can reach this conclusion by many routes. People can accept the equality of man because they believe that all men were created by God, they can believe it because they feel that the scientific evidence supports such a conclusion, or they can accept it simply because they believe it is the only basis on which life in society can be organized without injustice. It does not matter why people accept the equality of man as the basis of social organization; all that matters is that they do accept it.

This means that socialism cannot require that its adherents be atheists. There is not the slightest necessity for people to study metaphysics and decide whether there is one God, many Gods, or no God, before they can be socialist. It is not necessary to try and decide whether there is an after-life, or what kind, before you can be a socialist. These questions are important to man, but irrelevant to socialism; trying to bring them into the discussion about socialism simply causes quarrels between socialists, and thus weakens the struggle for the things they all support. What matters in socialism and to socialists is that you should care about a particular kind of social relationship on this earth. Why you care is your own affair. There is nothing incompatible between socialism and Christianity, Islam, or any other religion which accepts the equality of man on earth.

The fact that socialism and religion are two different things does not mean that socialism is anti-religious. In a socialist society the members of the community would be free to be religious, and to follow whatever religion they wish; the society would try very hard not to make a decision which outrages the religious feelings of any of its members, however small in numbers the group may be. There are times, however, when this cannot be done—for example if questions of public health arose in an urban society out of certain religious burial practices. But even then, every effort would be made to reach agreement with the people concerned; the religious feelings would always be taken into account.

This necessity for religious toleration arises out of the nature of socialism. For a man's religious beliefs are important to him, and the purpose of socialism is Man. Socialism does not just seek to serve some abstract thing called 'the people'; it seeks to maximize the benefit of society to all the individuals who are members of it. It is thus the essentially personal nature of religious beliefs which makes it necessary for socialism to leave religious questions alone as far as possible—which makes it necessary that socialism should be secular. And being secular involves trying to avoid upsetting deeply held religious beliefs however stupid they may appear to non-believers. The wearing of long hair, the erection of statues to the religious heroes or saints, the pouring of libations, the ban on music and dancing—all these things appear at best irrelevant to those who do not follow the religion concerned, but they are important to those who do. And because they are important to these believers, a socialist society will not interfere. It will not force people to cut their hair, nor allow others to be forced to wear their hair long. It will not prohibit libations, although it may ask that they be poured where they will not damage public property. It will not force people to dance, even if the society has agreed that its people should do a period of National Service which normally includes dance activity. It will protect the statues from wilful damage. It will allow genuine conscientious objection to the bearing of arms, and so on. Always socialism will try to enlarge freedom, and religious freedom is an essential part of man's liberty.

There is no Theology of Socialism

There is, however, an apparent tendency among certain socialists to try and establish a new religion—a religion of socialism itself. This is usually called 'scientific socialism' and the works of Marx and Lenin are regarded as the holy writ in the light of which all other thoughts and actions of socialists have to be judged.

Of course, this doctrine is not presented as a religion; its proponents are often most anxious to decry religion as the 'opium of the people', and they present their beliefs as 'science'. Yet they talk and act in the same manner as the most rigid of theologians. We find them condemning one another's actions because they do not accord with what the priests of 'scientific socialism' have decided is the true meaning, in modern terms, of books written more than 100 years ago. Indeed we are fast getting to the stage where quarrels between different Christian sects about the precise meaning of the Bible fade into insignificance when compared with the quarrels of those who claim to be the true interpreters of Marxism-Leninism!

This attempt to create a new religion out of socialism is absurd. It is not scientific, and it is almost certainly not Marxist—for however combatant and quarrelsome a socialist Marx was, he never claimed to be an infallible divinity! Marx was a great thinker. He gave a brilliant analysis of the industrial capitalist society in which he lived; he diagnosed its ills and advocated certain remedies which he believed would lead to the development of a healthy society. But he was not God. The years have proved him wrong in certain respects just as they have proved him right in others. Marx did not write revealed truth; his books are the result of hard thinking and hard work, not a revelation from God. It is therefore unscientific to appeal to his writings as Christians appeal to the Bible, or Muslims to the Koran.

The works of Marx and Lenin are useful to a socialist because these men thought about the objective conditions of their time and tried to work out the actions necessary to achieve certain ends. We can learn from their methods of analysis, and from their ideas. But the same is true of many other thinkers of the past. It is no part of the job of a socialist in 1968 to worry about whether or not his actions or proposals are in accordance with what Marx or Lenin wrote, and it is a waste of time and energy to spend hours— if not months and years—trying to prove that what you have decided is objectively necessary is really in accordance with their teachings. The task of a socialist is to think out for himself the best way of achieving desired ends under the conditions which exist now. It is his job to think how to organize society, how to solve a particular problem, or how to effect certain changes, in a manner which will emphasize the importance of man and the equality of man.

It is especially important that we in Africa should understand this. We are groping our way forward towards socialism, and we are in danger of being bemused by this new theology, and therefore of trying to solve our problems according to what the priests of Marxism say is what Marx said or meant. If we do this we shall fail. Africa's conditions are very different from those of the Europe in which Marx and Lenin wrote and worked. To talk as if these thinkers provided all the answers to our problems, or as if Marx invented socialism, is to reject both the humanity of Africa and the universality of socialism. Marx did contribute a great deal to socialist thought. But socialism did not begin with him, nor can it end in constant reinterpretations of his writings.

Speaking generally, and despite the existence of a few feudalistic communities, traditional Tanzanian society had many socialist characteristics. The people did not call themselves socialists, and they were not socialists by deliberate design. But all people were workers, there was no living off the sweat of others. There was no very great difference in the amount of goods available to the different members of the society. All these are socialist characteristics. Despite the low level of material progress, traditional African society was in practice organized on a basis which was in accordance with socialist principles.

These conditions still prevail over large areas of Tanzania—and indeed in many other parts of Africa. Even in our urban areas, the social expectation of sharing what you have with your kinsfolk is still very strong—and causes great problems for individuals! These things have nothing to do with Marx; the people have never heard of him. Yet they provide a basis on which modern socialism can be built. To reject this base is to accept the idea that Africa has nothing to contribute to the march of mankind; it is to argue that the only way progress can be achieved in Africa is if we reject our own past and impose on ourselves the doctrines of some other society.

Nor would it be very scientific to reject Africa's past when trying to build socialism in Africa. For scientific thinking means finding out all the facts in a particular situation, regardless of whether you like them or not, or whether they fit in with preconceived ideas. It means analysing these facts, and then working out solutions to the problems you are concerned with in the light of these facts, and of the objectives you are trying to achieve. This is what Marx did in Europe in the middle of the nineteenth century; if he had lived in Sukumaland, Masailand, or Ruvuma, he would have written a different book than Das Kapital, but he could have been just as scientific and just as socialist. For if 'scientific socialism' means anything, it can only mean that the objectives are socialist and you apply scientific methods of study in working out the appropriate policies. If the phrase does not mean that, then it is simply a trap to ensnare the unwary into a denunciation of their own nature and therefore into a new form of oppression. For a scientist works to discover truth. He does not claim to know it, nor is he seeking to discover truth as revealed—which is the job of the theologian. A scientist works on the basis of the knowledge which has been accumulated empirically, and which is held to be true until new experience demonstrates otherwise, or demonstrates a superior truth which takes precedence in particular situations.

A really scientific socialist would therefore start his analysis of the problems of a particular society from the standpoint of that society. In Tanzania he would take the existence of some socialist values as part of his material for analysis; he would study the effect of the colonial era on these attitudes and on the systems of social organization; he would take account of the world situation as it affects Tanzania. After doing all that he would try to work out policies appropriate for the growth of a modern socialist state. And he could well finish up with the Arusha Declaration and the policies of ujamaa!

A scientific socialist could do all this with or without a knowledge and understanding of Marx and Lenin—or for that matter Saint-Simon, Owen or Laski. Knowledge of the work and thinking of these and other people may help a socialist to know what to look for and how to evaluate the things he sees; but it could also mislead him if he is not careful. Equally, a knowledge of history may help him to learn from the experience of others; a knowledge of economics will help him to understand some of the forces at work in the society. But if he tries to use any of these disciplines or philosophies as a gospel according to which he must work cut solutions he will go wrong. There is no substitute for his own hard work and hard thinking.

For example, a study of the work of past socialist thinkers and of history and economics appears to have led some people to argue that Tanzania can only become socialist if it first goes through the stage of capitalism. Yet it is difficult to believe that they thought about the objective conditions of this country when coming to this conclusion. (It is also difficult to believe that they understand the principles of socialism—the attitude of mind it requires!) Certainly Tanzania was part of the Western capitalist world while it was under colonial domination, but it was very much on the fringe. Certainly our independent nation inherited a few capitalist institutions, and some of our people adopted capitalist and individualistic ideas as a result of their education or their envy of the colonial representatives whom they encountered. But the masses of the people did not become capitalist, and are not filled with capitalist ideas. By far the largest part of our economy is not organized on capitalist lines. Indeed, whenever we try to help Africans to become capitalist shopkeepers, capitalist farmers, industrialists, etc., we find that most of them fail because they cannot adopt the capitalist practices which are essential to commercial success! Yet rather than give up their theories, these dogmatists often attribute these African failures to the machinations of a racial minority—thus revealing their racialism and non-socialist beliefs—instead of recognizing that capitalism demands certain attributes among its practitioners which the majority of our people have never been forced to acquire.

Under these circumstances what would be the sense in working to create capitalism, with all the individualism, social aggressiveness, and human indignities which it involves? These attributes would have to be fought against, and the organizations of capitalism destroyed or reformed, when you finally decided that the task of building socialism could be begun. And when should opposition to capitalism be started? If capitalism must precede socialism, how far does it have to go before it can be replaced?

Capitalism would only have to precede socialism if there was some reason to believe that the people will fail to solve the problems of production except by capitalist methods. It is certainly true that capitalism can lead to the high output of goods and services—no socialist would dispute that. But there is very little evidence to support the contention that only through capitalism can a satisfactory level of production be attained; indeed there is an increasing amount of evidence with which to refute such a statement. Countries like the USSR, East Germany, China, and North Korea may differ in their approach to socialism, but they are certainly not capitalist, and they do produce the goods their people need. North Korea, for example, may not be able to compare with the state of New York in the provision of television sets, cars, and fashion clothes; but it has electrified something like 98 per cent of its villages, and 86 per cent of its farm houses, and it has built new and improved houses for about two thirds of its rural families in the space of eight years. In other words, the priorities of production may be different, and the emphasis given to economic output as against other values may vary, but North Korea has shown that production can be organized in a non-capitalist manner. If it can be done once, what reason is there to believe that it cannot be done again?

The real truth is that the principles of socialism are relevant to all human society at all stages of technology and social organization. But their application has constantly to be worked out afresh according to the objective conditions prevailing in the time or place. There is no book which provides all the answers to these problems of application; there is no 'socialist road map' which depicts all obstacles and provides a path through or around them. In fact we have no alternative but to hold fast to the principles of socialism— to understand its characteristics—and then apply the accumulated knowledge of man to the continuing and changing problems of man. And we have to do this as best we can, without the infinite knowledge which belongs to God and which would provide the answers to all our problems. There is no magic formula, and no short cut to socialism. We can only grope our way forward, doing our best to think clearly—and scientifically—about our own conditions in relation to our objectives.

There is No Model for Us to Copy

In 1965 Tanzania adopted its own form of democracy—we rejected the Western model and said it was not appropriate for our circumstances despite the fact that all our constitutional development had until then been based on it. We looked at different democratic systems round the world, and studied the work of different thinkers, and we asked ourselves two questions. First, what is the purpose of democratic systems? And second, what are the conditions of Tanzania, and what special problems face the country? Then we worked out a system of one-party Government which seemed to us to include the essential elements of democracy at the same time as it provided for unity and strength in Government, and took account of our poverty, our size, our traditions, and our aspirations. The resultant constitution is not perfect; but it suits us better than any system operating elsewhere, and we believe that it safeguards the people's sovereignty at the same time as it enables the effective and strong Government so essential at this stage of our development.

When we introduced this new system, we were criticized for 'abandoning democracy', and even now these charges are still heard. The criticisms came mostly from the traditional democracies of the West; even some of our sympathizers felt that we had taken a step backwards in our development. In response to this criticism we tried to explain what we were trying to do and why we thought our new system was both democratic and suitable for our conditions. But having done that we did not worry about what the Western countries said or what democratic theorists said. For in rejecting the idea that we had to follow the 'Westminster model' if we wanted to be democratic, we had also overcome the psychological need to have a certificate of approval from the West in relation to our political system. We did not reject this idea of an accolade from the West because we were critical of the political systems operating in Western countries. On the contrary, there was much that we admired in them, and we learned a great deal from them. But we acted as intelligent and thoughtful citizens of Tanzania who wanted democracy to be a continuing reality in our own country.

What we have done in relation to democracy we have also to do in relation to socialism. It is not intelligent to reject an accolade from the West on democracy in order to seek one from the East on socialism. Socialism is about people, and people are the products of their history, education, and environment. It is absurd to assume that while democracy has to be adapted to the circumstances of the country in order that the people's will shall be effective, socialism can just be copied from somewhere else. Admiration of some facets of democracy in Britain, Sweden, and elsewhere did not lead us to imitation. Equally we should be able to admire certain things which have been done in China, Russia, Korea, Yugoslavia, and so on, without assuming that any of these countries provide a model for us to copy.

Unfortunately some of our people—often the ones who were most insistent that we should not copy the democracy of the West—are now judging our socialist policies and progress by what Moscow or Peking have done, and are demanding that we do something because it has proved useful in one of these places. They get upset if the communist parties of these countries express disapproval (either explicitly or implicitly), because they believe that the model for socialism already exists there, and that we can only be really socialist if we have earned a 'certificate of approval' from the guardians of this model. Such people are refusing to think for themselves. They are saying that the perfect answer to the problems of man in society is already known, and all we have to do is to copy others. Once again, they arc saying that Africa has nothing to contribute to the world and all good things come from elsewhere. And then, in their insecurity, they look for a 'certificate of socialist approval' from the country or party which they believe has these answers.

We must avoid this attitude. It is neither patriotic nor sensible to deny the need for Western approval and in the next breath to seek an accolade from the East. Tanzania does not need a certificate of approval about its internal policies from any outside group. The only approval our policies need is the approval of the Tanzanian people. We shall get that if we succeed in dealing with our own problems in a way which is suitable to our present circumstances and acceptable to the people's beliefs and understanding at any one time. True Tanzanians will worry about what the Tanzanian people think, not what anyone else thinks. True Tanzanian socialists will worry about how the Tanzanian people can move in the quickest possible time towards a society where socialist principles find their fullest expression. They will not worry about the approval or disapproval of other socialists in matters which are of exclusive concern to us.

Of course it would be stupid to allow an insistence on working out our own policies to develop into a rejection of the lessons we can learn from the experiences of other countries and the ideas of other people. To say that Tanzania does not need certificates of approval from this country or that does not mean that we cannot learn from non-Tanzanians. This kind of automatic rejection of something because it is said by an American or Chinese, or done in Britain or Poland, is as much a reflection of an inferiority complex as the automatic acceptance of what they say or do.

Why should Tanzania not learn from the agricultural communes of China? Their experience could promote thought and ideas about our own rural organization, provided that we go to learn, and proceed to think—not to copy. Why can we not learn from the Korean success in rural transformation in comparison with continuing difficulties in other Communist countries? Do the Cuban experiments in adult education have nothing to teach us? Agricultural organization, rural transformation, adult education, are all problems we have to deal with in Tanzania; why should we not study the techniques used by other men to see if they could usefully be adapted to meet our needs, or if they provide a clue to the solution of a difficulty we are experiencing?

Nor do we have to confine our attention to development in communist countries. The co-operative settlements of Israel, the co-operative organizations of Denmark and Sweden, have all accumulated great experience which we could learn from. Even the most avowedly capitalist countries have something to teach us— for example, the techniques by which they encourage workers to increase their output. We do not have to adopt these blindly, but we could usefully consider whether, or to what extent, these techniques are acceptable to a socialist society. And what of the freedom for individuals to express their beliefs and ideas about government, about policies, about organization? Is there nothing valuable for us in this freedom? Even if individual freedom to vote and organize does not have the exclusive importance which advocates of capitalism appear to give it, surely it is a reflection of one facet of man's equality and therefore important to a socialist? How far can we achieve this kind of freedom and equality in our circumstances without sacrificing other freedoms and equalities?

We in Tanzania are a part of mankind. We have to take our place in the world. We would be stupid to reject everything or everyone coming out of the West because that is the home of capitalism; we would be stupid to reject everything the communists do. We are trying to build ujamaa—socialism—which is neither of these things. We can learn from both—and from other political systems—without trying to copy or seeking for their approval. Our task is to look first at our own position and our own needs, and then to consider other experience and other suggestions in the light of our requirements. We should not put ourselves into blinkers as though we were a horse which could not be trusted to see what is going on elsewhere. We should be willing to learn from our fellow men, and we should contribute to the common pool of knowledge and experience. We can do this if we use our brains—that is, if we THINK.

The Universality and Diversity of Socialism

What does all this amount to? It is an expression of belief that man can only live in harmony with man, and can only develop to his full potential as a unique individual, in a society the purpose of which is Man, which is based on the principles of human equality, and which is so organized as to emphasize both man's equality and his control over all the instruments of his life and development.

It is a statement that because men are different, and because different communities and societies have had different histories, live in different geographical conditions, and have developed different customs and systems of belief, therefore the road to socialism and the institutions through which socialism is ultimately expressed will be different. It is a statement insisting that the progress of one man or group of men does not make it unnecessary for other men and other groups to think for themselves. It is an assertion that there are no natural laws of human development which we have only to discover and apply in order to reach the Nirvana of a perfect socialist society; on the contrary, that it is by deliberate design that men will build socialist societies, and by deliberate design that they will maintain socialist principles in a form which seems to them to be good. It is an assertion of man's unity and also his diversity; the validity of certain basic principles for social living, and the variety of their expression. It is a statement that one will not recognize or define a socialist society by its institutions or its statements, but by its fundamental characteristics of equality, cooperation, and freedom.

The Transition to Socialism

By definition, however, the characteristics which identify a socialist state will not exist in their entirety in a state which is trying to build socialism. If the institutions, and the attitudes, of socialism existed it would be socialist; until then it is inevitable that at least some of the essential elements of socialist society will be missing. This is true whether the commitment to socialism is linked with revolution, or whether it follows peaceful political development.

Socialism does not spring ready-made out of the womb of violence. Even the most successful and popular revolution inevitably leaves behind it a legacy of bitterness, suspicion and hostility between members of the society. These are not conducive to the institutions of equality, and make it difficult to build a spirit of co-operation between the whole people. In particular there is always a fear that those who suffered during the revolution may be looking for an opportunity of revenge; there is the memory of injury and bereavement deliberately inflicted, which poisons the relations between men within the society. A violent revolution may make the introduction of socialist *institutions* easier; it makes more difficult the development of the socialist *attitudes* which give life to these institutions.

This is not to say that violent revolutions are always wrong or irrelevant to socialism. Sometimes they are a regrettable necessity because they are the only way to break the power of those who prevent progress towards socialism. But violence is a short cut only to the destruction of the institutions and power groups of the old society; they are not a short cut to the building of the new. For even if change is secured through the violent overthrow of a feudal or a fascist society, the new life has still to be built by and with people who lived in the old society and who were shaped by it even if they reacted against it. The necessity for a violent revolution brings its own problems to the building of socialism; they may be different problems from those experienced by the states which are fortunate enough to be able to move peacefully from one kind of social system to another, but they are nonetheless real.

In fact those who talk as if violence must always and everywhere precede socialism, and who judge a country to be developing towards socialism only if violence has occurred, are almost certainly not socialist in their own attitudes. For violence cannot be welcomed by those who care about people. It is a very serious matter because of the misery and suffering it involves for human beings; it should only be accepted as a necessity when every other road forward is completely blocked and cannot be cleared by persistence, by public determination, or by other expressions of the majority will. Violence itself is the opposite of a socialist characteristic. Brigands can govern by violence and fear; dictatorships can establish themselves and flourish. Socialism cannot be imposed in this way, for it is based on equality. It denies the right of any individual or any small minority, to say, 'I know and the others are fools who must be led like sheep'. Leadership can be given—and indeed must be given— in a socialist state. But it must be the people's leadership, which they accept because ultimately they control it. Socialist leadership is of the people; it cannot be imposed by force or tyranny.

This means that where a violent revolution was a necessary precondition for the establishment of an opportunity to begin the work of building socialism, the early period of transition towards this goal will have certain kinds of non-socialist characteristics. There may well be suspicions, fear, illegalities, and an absence of political freedom; there may be something of a vacuum in effective administration even as brave attempts are made to create the groundwork of socialist economic organizations.

If, on the other hand, the transition out of the old society can be effected by non-violent means, different non-socialist characteristics will be evident as the work of building is in process. There will be many remnants of the preceding social organization; many old habits may continue simply because social upheaval has not forced people to think about them; and old attitudes and behaviour may still be dominant in people holding responsible positions. These things create difficulties for socialist progress just as the aftermath of a revolution creates difficulties. By whichever method the conditions or building socialism are established, a visitor could look at the society in transition and deny its socialism, or its progress, by pointing to characteristics which are non-socialist, or even anti-socialist.

This is as true in Tanzania as elsewhere, and indeed our Union provides examples of the difficulties of both kinds of transition. In Zanzibar the revolution cleared many obstacles from the path of socialism, but it created other difficulties and fears. On the mainland, where political circumstances obviated the necessity for violence, we are able to try to build socialism by evolution—by dealing with the problems one by one in accordance with the consensus of opinion and our capacity at any one time. But this, too, has its difficulties, and the danger that self-seeking men will be able to mislead the people into opposing the struggle forward. And in both parts of the Union we have still to ensure that new privileged groups do not grow out of the post-independence and post-revolutionary forces.

The solution to all these problems depends upon the growth of socialist understanding and socialist attitudes among the people. In particular it depends upon the speed and success with which the concepts of human equality and the people's sovereignty are accepted by the society and the leadership in the society. Institutions can help to spread these ideas and encourage their expression, but they do not in themselves provide an answer. Thus, for example, the Permanent Commission of Enquiry provides machinery through which members of the public can complain against petty tyranny of leaders and officials, but its effectiveness depends upon the willingness of the people to make and to substantiate their complaints, as well as the willingness of Government and Party personnel to correct wrongs which reduce the people's sovereignty. Or, again, the leadership qualifications are aimed at emphasizing the identity of the leadership and the people, but they can only restrict behaviour negatively—and their intentions can be evaded. There is, in fact, no substitute for the individual moral courage of men; everything ultimately depends upon the determination of the people to be judges over those to whom they have entrusted positions of responsibility and leadership. The only way in which leadership can be maintained as a people's leadership is if the leaders have reason to fear the judgement of the people.

The people's purposes in society, however, will only go forward smoothly when they exercise their power over leadership in a calm and deliberate manner—and when the institutions of the society enable them to do so. And the people have to understand their own power, and its importance to their future; they have to understand the basic principles of socialism. Only then will they be able to avoid being used by the jealousies and envies of individuals who seek to exploit, for their own ambition's sake, the honest mistakes of individual leaders. Only then will the people be able to avoid the blandishments of those who, for their own benefit, pretend that there is a short cut to socialism and to prosperity which the existing leaders stand in the way of. The people's will must be sovereign; but it will only lead them to the equalities and dignities of socialism if they exert that sovereignty with an understanding of socialism.

The Problems of Building Socialism in an Ex-Colonial Country

There are particular problems about this in an ex-colonial country like Tanzania. For to build socialism you must have socialists— particularly in leading positions. It is not enough that our people's traditional life should have been based upon socialist principles; that is good, but it is necessary that the leaders in modernization should also accept those principles and be able to apply them in the very different technological and international conditions of the twentieth century. Further, it is essential that the people should be aware of the new socialist objective and what it means to them.

Yet in Tanzania the great mass campaigns of the 1950s and early 1960s were for independence. We campaigned against colonialism, against foreign domination. We did not campaign against capitalism or for socialism. Creating still more difficulties was the fact that the colonialism we fought against was that of a people who happened to be of a different racial group than ourselves. It was fatally easy to identify the thing you were fighting against as people of this other race—the Europeans. It is true that we in Tanzania campaigned on the grounds of human equality; that has helped us. But the problem Africa knew was that of discrimination against the African majority. We therefore asked, 'Why are there no African District Commissioners, administrators, supervisors, secretaries, etc.?', and often this was transposed into, 'Why are there European or Asian—this and that?' Humanity took second place in this struggle very often; even when political leaders said on public platforms and elsewhere that they would never countenance reverse discrimination after independence, this was sometimes interpreted as a manoeuvre designed to avoid the heavy hand of the colonial authority! Almost throughout Africa, therefore, the first and most vocal demand of the people after independence was for Africanization. They did not demand localization—indeed, the most popular thing would have been for leaders to deny citizenship to non-black residents. Still less did the people demand socialization; they simply demanded the replacement of white and brown faces by black ones. The leaders could therefore receive applause if they replaced white, or brown, capitalists by black ones. Capitalism was the system which the masses knew in the modern sector, and what they had been fighting against was that this modern sector should be in alien hands.

It was not only the masses who looked upon things in this way; many leaders of the independence struggle themselves saw things in these terms. They were not against capitalism; they simply wanted its fruits, and saw independence as the means to that end. Indeed, many of the most active fighters in the independence movement were motivated—consciously or unconsciously—by the belief that only with independence could they attain that ideal of individual wealth which their education or their experience in the modern sector had established as a worthwhile goal. It is in this fact that lies the paradox of the changing classifications given to different African leaders by the capitalists of the colonial territories. For the 'extremist' of the independence period was sometimes the man who was saying, 'Kill the whites' because he wanted what they had for himself. In such a case (if he survives) the 'extremist' may well become a great defender of capitalism after independence, and he will then probably be reclassified as a 'moderate'! Similarly, the independence campaigner who opposed the murder of non-Africans could either have been deeply religious, or he could have been a socialist. If he was the latter, his classification by the capitalists after independence is liable to change from 'moderate' to 'extremist' or 'communist'!

This lack of ideological content during the independence struggle often served to maintain unity among the anti-colonialist forces, or to prevent a diversion of energies into the difficult questions of socialist education. (It was not always selfishness which made leaders think only in terms of Africanizing the capitalist economy. Often they had no knowledge of any alternative). But it can present a serious problem in the post-independence period. Once they have power, some of the leaders whom the people have learned to know and trust will think their nationalism demands expropriation of non-Africans in favour of African citizens; the sophisticated may deny this but think of economic development in terms of expanding capitalism with the participation of Africans.

Such leaders as these may well identify the progress they have promised the people with the increasing wealth of the few; they will point to African-owned large cars and luxurious houses, and so on, as evidence of growing prosperity and of their own devotion to the cause of national independence. It was on this basis, for example, that some Tanzanian leaders criticized the Arusha Declaration. They said that the leadership qualifications prevented Africans from becoming landowners and businessmen, while Asians and Europeans could continue in these fields as they had done before independence. These critics thus demonstrated their conviction, firstly, that Asian citizens could not or should not desire to hold responsible positions in the society; and secondly, that exploitation was only wrong when carried out upon the masses by people of a different race. Incidentally, they were also showing that they wished to use positions of power for private gain, because almost the only way in which Africans could get the capital to become landlords or capitalists was by virtue of their office or their seniority in the public service. (There were exceptions to this general rule, because there had been isolated instances before independence of Africans establishing themselves in business or modern farming. But in general it was the post-independence accession to power which enabled Africans to enter the capitalist system as owners or employers instead of as workers).

The perpetuation of capitalism, and its expansion to include Africans, will be accepted by the masses who took part in the independence struggle. They may take the new wealth of their leaders as natural and even good—for a time they may even take a reflected pride in it. This may go on for a long period if economic circumstances of the country allow a simultaneous lightening of the general poverty—or even if the conditions of the masses remain static. This public acceptance of African capitalism will be obtained because the people have learned to trust their nationalist leaders, and will wish to honour them. Also there will inevitably be new jobs and opportunities for a good number of the most active, vocal and intelligent of those who might otherwise have led criticism. And on top of that, there will be an end to stupidities like interference with traditional African customs by a foreign Government. But, sooner or later, the people will lose their enthusiasm and will look upon the independence Government as simply another new ruler which they should avoid as much as possible. Provided it has been possible to avoid any fundamental upset in their traditional economic and social conditions, they will then sink back into apathy—until the next time someone is able to convince them that their own efforts can lead to an improvement in their lives!

It is comparatively easy to get independence from a colonial power—especially one which claims to base its national morality on the principles of freedom and democracy. Everyone wants to be free, and the task of a nationalist is simply to rouse the people to a confidence in their own power of protest. But to build the real freedom which socialism represents is a very different thing. It demands a positive understanding and positive actions, not simply a rejection of colonialism and a willingness to co-operate in non-co-operation. And the anti-colonial struggle will almost certainly have intensified the difficulties.

During the campaign for independence a number of developments were probably inevitable, or were unavoidable except at great cost. First, is the fact that racialism has been allowed to grow—and may even have been indirectly encouraged during the process of simplifying the issues at stake. In Tanzania the masses remained remarkably free from this disease—and are still free. But many of the leaders suffered from discrimination themselves, and some have been unable to achieve that degree of objectivity which would enable them to direct their hatred towards discrimination itself instead of at the racial group which the discriminators represented. Yet racialism is absolutely and fundamentally contrary to the first principle of socialism—the equality of man.

Second, the most active, and therefore the most popular, of the nationalist leaders may have been people without a socialist conviction. They may either have never had an opportunity to study the problems and possibilities of social and economic organization, or they may even have been people who were motivated by a personal desire for the fruits of capitalism.

Third, all the national Party organization and education were geared to defeating colonialism and to opposing people of another race who happened to be in positions of power. This means that once independence is achieved, and the key positions of power have been Africanized, there is a grave danger that the Party will lose support and will atrophy. The people—and even many of the leaders—may feel that the Party has achieved its purpose; once independence has been attained there is no point in the effort required to sustain it.

All these things mean that after independence the work of building socialism has to be started from the beginning. The people have to be shown another goal—the goal of socialism—and they have to learn that only by extending their efforts for this second purpose will they really benefit from the effort they have already made.

To do this new task a strong Party organization is as essential as it was before independence, but it involves a serious and conscious effort on the part of the leaders. In particular they have to act deliberately so as to emphasize their identification with the people, and so as to remain one of them. During the independence struggle this was no problem: the leaders lived with the people, and were as poor as the masses whom they led. They had no choice in the matter and no particular temptation. In the struggle for socialism the position is different: often the leaders have to live in more comfortable surroundings if they are to do their new Government tasks efficiently, and they are also faced with all the temptations of power. Yet to be effective leaders in this second phase of the freedom struggle, it is essential that they should turn their backs on these temptations; they have to act like socialists and be prepared to account to the people for all the personal wealth which they deploy.

However, it is not only leaders who must be involved in the building of socialism. There must be an active adult education system which is directed at helping the people to understand the principles of socialism and their relevance to real development and freedom. There must be local institutions of socialism—co-operative societies which are under the effective control of the members, ujamaa villages, and so on. These are as essential to the building of ujamaa as the Government action which secures control of the key points of the economy for the people at the same time as it mobilizes all the resources of skill and experience which are available. In addition, new economic, social and political institutions must be created which will stress the equality of all men regardless of race or tribe, and which will enable the people to make their voices heard throughout the society. Yet all this must be done under conditions which safeguard these infant institutions, and the young state, from subversion. These things must be achieved while the people are protected against the manipulation of those who are so arrogant that they wish to enforce their own judgement of what is 'the good life'.

This is a formidable—though not exhaustive—list of work to be done even when stated in such broad and general terms. It becomes much more difficult when translated into practice—when you begin to work out the details which appear insignificant but which can make all the difference to success or failure. The difficulties are exacerbated in Africa where the responsibilities and temptations of new nationhood coincide with a great shortage of educated people, of finance, and of committed, modern, and thinking socialists. But these same difficulties also provide unique opportunities. Because a new nation has been created, the people are ready and anxious for change—they only need leadership based on human respect. And the absence of large financial resources—once it is understood and accepted—forces a concentration on the abilities and the importance of men rather than money, and thus orientates the society towards the development of man instead of material wealth. The very magnitude of the problem creates a challenge, and the major difficulty is to relate the hard, detailed work, and the long-drawn-out struggle forward, to the ultimate goal.

In Tanzania we have begun the work of building socialism. So far all that we have really achieved is some success in showing people that there is another goal to work for now that our independence exists. For the rest we have tried to prevent the growth of new and stronger groups with a vested interest in capitalism; we have established some of the institutions through which the people can speak; and we have just begun to search out and help the local experiments in modern socialism. We have defined our policies in education, in rural development, and have listed our expectations of leadership. But we are NOT a socialist society. Our work has only just begun. Of particular priority are the outstanding tasks of socialist adult education, and of strengthening the people's self-confidence and pride. These are the essential preliminaries to real freedom from the abuse of power, and from the dangers of manipulation by ambitious, dishonest, and selfish men. They are also fundamental to the people's active participation in, and control of, the development of a new society.

The ultimate success in the work of building socialism in Tanzania—as elsewhere—depends upon the people of this nation. For any society is only what the people make it. The benefit to the people of a socialist society will depend upon their contribution to it—their work, their co-operation for the common good, and their acceptance of each other as equals and brothers.

To the extent that we in Tanzania succeed in the struggle to which we have committed ourselves, so we shall be taking our place in the march of humanity towards peace and human dignity. For too long we in Africa—and Tanzania as part of Africa—have slept, and allowed the rest of the world to walk round and over us. Now we are beginning to wake up and to join with our fellow human beings in deciding the destiny of the human race. By thinking out our own problems on the basis of those principles which have universal validity, Tanzania will make its contribution to the development of mankind. That is our opportunity and our responsibility.

August 1968

J.K.N.

INDEX

African Diaspora, 13, 82
African languages, 1-13, 65-66, 74
    Gikuyu, 2, 10, 13
    Swahili, 8, 10, 70, 92, 112
    Kiswahili, 65
African National Congress (ANC), 74, 78, 82, 102-07
    Freedom Charter (1955) of, 103
    Reconstruction and Development Programme (RDP) of, 102-03
"African socialism", 16, 47, 68, 90
Akivaga, Kichamu: expulsion of in 1970, 21
Amin, Idi, 54, 70-71
Angola, 22
Arusha Declaration, The, 30-32, 91, 112, 119, 126, 137
Asmara Declaration, 1-13
    Nyerere's influence on, 5

Babu, Mohamed, 22-23
Bretton Woods institutions, 32, 56, 73, 83
Britain. *See* colonialism.

capitalism, 17-18, 30-36, 66, 73-78, 90, 127-28, 136-41
Chama Chu Mapindazi (CCM), 36
China. *See* People's Republic of China.
Churchill, Winston, 15
"Club of Presidents", 22, 74
colonialism, 5-8, 10-12, 17, 28-29, 31, 68, 71-73, 136-41
    education system during, 88-90
    "Fabian", 22, 74
        Nyerere's aversion to, 41
Cooperative Movement (CM), 35
corporatism, 34-36, 72-73

Dar es Salaam, 16, 22, 24, 31, 53, 56, 69, 78
    University of, 21, 25, 45, 52n. 17, 67, 69
    decentralization project, 33-34

"democratic one-party state", 20, 23, 44-46, 51n. 14, 75, 79, 129-30
Democratic Republic of Congo (DRC), 8, 71

East African Common Services Organization (EACSO), 29
East African Community (EAC), 29
East African High Commission, 29
education, 8-12, 17, 23, 137
    during colonialism, 88-90
    Nyerere's critical education thought, 89-93
Engels, Friedrich, 97
Eritrea, 1-2, 10, 74
Ethiopia, 10, 74
exchange rate policy, 54, 56

Fanon, Frantz, 16
Financial Stability Forum, 59
FRELIMO, 20, 25

Germany, 31, 128
Group of Twenty (G20), 59

"humane governance", 60n. 5

International Monetary Fund, 19, 32, 49, 55, 58, 77, 83

Jamal, Amir, 55-56

Keita, Modibo, 72
Kenya, 2-3, 29, 71
    Masai people of, 9-10, 74
    Oromo people of, 10
    Somali people of, 10
Keynesianism, 105
Kivukoni College, 69

Leninism, 21, 44-45, 62, 124-25, 127

Lynch, William (American slave owner), 6-8

Machel, Samora, 20, 72
Mandela, Nelson: comparison of with Nyerere, 101-07, 108nn. 3, 5
Maoism, 45, 62
Marxism, 62, 97, 108n. 3, 124-27
Masai people, 9-10
Mbeki, Thabo: comparison of with Nyerere, 101-07
McNamara, Robert, 56
Mkapa, Benjamin, 57
Mondlane, Eduardo: successor to, 20
Mount Carmel Rubber Factory: arrest of workers at in 1973, 23
Mozambique, 20, 37
Mugabe, Robert, 102
Museveni, Yoweri, 65
Mwongozo, 23

National Assembly (Tanzania), 41, 43-45
National Executive Committee (Tanzania), 30, 44-45, 51n. 15
nationalism, 15-17, 20, 35
North Korea, 30, 128, 130-31
Nyerere, Julius K.: as democrat, 19-25; as nationalist, 15-17; as socialist, 17-19, 111-41; aversion of to colonialism, 41; Catholicism of, 36-37, 49n. 2, 66, 74; commitment of to equality for all, 41-42, 114-15, 139; commitment of to welfare of people, 39-49; comparison of with Mbeki and Mandela, 101-07; critical education thought of, 87-97; daughter of, 19; decentralization project of, 33-34; development of Tanzania under, 27-31, 67; "Economic Nationalism", 17-18; economic policies of, 53-59; *Education for Self-Reliance*, 17, 90, 92; emphasis of on self-reliance, 7-8, 31, 58, 64, 72-73; funeral of, 39-40; influence of on Asmara Declaration, 5; intellectual legacy of, 93-97; interest of in China, 30, 45, 62, 128, 130-31; leadership of, 63-65; obituaries for, 54; "Our Leadership and the Destiny

of Tanzania", 79; politics of Tanzania under, 32-36; *Socialism and Rural Development* of, 17; socialist programme of, 55, 66, 67, 71-72; translation of Shakespeare by, 8; *Uhuru na Ujamaa: Freedom and Socialism*, 111-41; undemocratic politics of, 22-25, 75. *See also* ujamaa; villagization.

Obote, Milton, 71
Official development assistance (ODA), 67-68
Organization of African Unity, 13, 16, 70
Oromo people, 10

PAFMECSA, 16
People's Republic of China, 30, 45, 62, 128, 130-31
Permanent Commission of Enquiry, 135

Reagan-Thatcher economics, 56
Reconstruction and Development Programme (RDP), 102-03
Rhodesia: independence of from Britain, 31
Ruvuma Development Association (RDA), 23-25, 65, 69-70, 75-76
Rwanda, 71

Sankara, Thomas, 72
self-reliance: Nyerere's emphasis on, 7-8, 31, 58, 64
Shakespeare, William: translation of into Swahili, 8
Shaw, George Bernard, 21
Simango: defeat of, 20
Smith, Ian, 31
Somalia, 10
Soros, George, 104-05
South Africa, 16, 82, 101-07
South African Communist Party, 106
Soviet Union (USSR), 105, 128, 130
Sudan, 10
SWAPO, 22, 74

Tanganyika, 31, 41, 44, 50n. 3, 68, 88-89, 112